Single Truth

You are more than your relationship status

Annie Harton, MA, LMFTA

DEDICATION

To my first love

LETTER OF DEDICATION

To my first love,

I thank you for loving me enough to break up with me. I was blessed with the time to grow into myself and embrace my season of singleness. Everything happens in God's perfect timing and I know that this is no exception. If we had gotten married when we planned to, I would likely still have my identity in being your girl, instead of as God's daughter. Our breakup was the turning point in my story.

My heart has been convicted to write for others so that they can know God's love and value in the season they are in. There has not been a day that has gone by that I haven't prayed for you and your journey toward sanctity. It is through your example of faith that I have grown to be more courageous and confident in the existence of God. I am confident that His merciful love has led us to taste each fruit (whether sweet or sour) at the perfect time. God doesn't work in any other way than by offering perfect goodness.

Though I resisted the breakup the whole first year, I have begun to know and love the cross more intimately. Loving you from afar has been neither easy nor preferred, but it has taught me about sacrificial love and how God longs for each of us. I pray that you know that you are worthy of love and you recognize it when you find it. You were the greatest thing that ever happened to me. I will be forever grateful for the memories and lessons I learned in our season.

Love,
Annie

CONTENTS

LETTER TO THE READER

Friend,

Thank you for picking up this book. Though I've been writing it for only a short time, I've been living the story for years. It is natural for me to live with my heart on my sleeve, but it definitely pokes at my pride to put it on the page. I'm guessing that you picked up this book because you are either looking for some hope in a season of singleness or curious to know what a single marriage counselor could know about love. Whether you're single or married, I hope this book helps to remind you that God's plan for you is perfect and your relationship status does not influence His love for you. Each day of our lives is filled with emotional experiences and insights that help us to see glimpses of God's love story with us. The Psalms are a beautiful way to express the variety of emotions we feel in this life. If you don't feel worthy of love, I hope this book can tackle some of the lies that you are believing. I hope these chapters will invite you to find truth in your own story and see how God is leading your heart. You are priceless and that's the truth!

With a grateful heart praying for you,
Annie

SINGLE TRUTH: MY STORY

Single.

It is a word I identified with for a quarter of a century. When I was 25 years old, I received my first-ever wedding invitation with a "plus one." Everything was about to change.

One of my college roommates would be marrying her groom in Chicago and our other roomies would attend with their long-term boyfriends. I began praying my favorite 30-day prayer to St. Joseph for the right man to invite. I didn't want to be the odd one out *again* without a date. And, at my age, I didn't just want a guy friend to tagalong. I was shooting for the moon and praying for a forever date. As the RSVP deadline approached without any prospect in sight, I begrudgingly sent in my response as a party of one. I guess it *still* was not God's time for me to have a partner on the dance floor at a wedding reception.

On the 30th day of my prayer, a guy I recently met appeared on my summer kickball roster. We had met at the door at a young adult gathering two months before. He was wearing a bright red Coca-Cola T-shirt and his handsome eyes and adorable smile immediately drew me in. I was not able to stop staring at him for a few long minutes. I took this time to process what my mind, heart, and soul were piecing together in this real-life "meet cute" happening before my eyes. It was weird how different this guy seemed. Was this what they call "love at first sight"?

We learned that we played in the same volleyball league, but our teams had not faced one another on the court. The gathering we attended was a mixer for all volleyball players to socialize with members from other teams in the league. After we dominated as partners in Euchre (a popular card game in the Midwest) that night, he forgot to ask for my number. Before we parted ways, I told him that I was selling tickets to a gala that was quickly approaching. He bought an individual ticket from me—which communicated to me that he was single and interested. He never showed. With no contact information, he became a mystery man.

What a surprise to see him on the 30th day! He must be the answer to my prayer!

Without hesitation, I asked him to get a beer after the first kickball game. My plan to spend time with him alone was altered as another teammate joined us. It was awkward to have a third wheel, but I had been in that position many times before. It was cute that he was trying to direct his attention toward me as much as possible. I was for once *not* the third wheel.

As soon as I got home that evening, I called the bride and explained that I was hoping this budding friendship would progress into more before the wedding. With only a few weeks before the big day, she was already finalizing the number of guests. The clock was ticking. If I was going to switch my RSVP, I'd have to ask him ASAP. I was going to do what I needed to do to ask this guy to her wedding.

Even though I have been encouraged to be a leader in the world as a proud alumna of an all-women's college, I believe a woman's heart is made to be pursued. Making the first move is not what I had dreamed, but I did not want this opportunity to be lost. I often join my dad, my uncle, and a couple of his best friends at a spin class on Monday evenings before enjoying a craft beer at the brewery down the street. I considered this to be a natural way to ask him out for a beer since I was already planning on being there. Less than 24 hours after our first beer, this invitation would surely scare him away. I would seem too desperate and too eager. I couldn't believe that I wanted a wedding date so badly that I would risk losing a friendship I had just found!

Now that we had exchanged numbers, I casually texted him about the opportunity to check out this brewery he had never been to. When my phone dinged, I was shocked by his "yes!" I was full of excitement and hope! I was not able to rest long in his "yes" before I grew nervous about how and when to invite him to the wedding. I started to doubt my great idea about initiating a "first date" with so much at stake while the others from my spin class were tables away. I often come straight from the workout to enjoy the well-deserved, refreshing libation, but on this special occasion I showered at the gym. I wanted to look my best!

For the second day in a row, my plan was altered as he thought it would be fun to sit with my spin-class group. I failed to mention to him who was at the table and did not know how to spontaneously introduce him to my dad, so I waited until halfway through our pints to do so.

He not only remained at the table after the unconventional introduction, but also asked if I wanted to get dinner with him at the pizzeria next door. I could not believe he had not run away yet! This was all too good to be true. Did I really have to risk asking him to the wedding?

Over pizza, as the hours passed by, we discovered more and more things that we had in common. I was thrilled to look across the table into his eyes and share a sense of humor. We made one another laugh. That was important for me. As servers were closing out checks and cleaning off tables around us, I knew it was time to ask about the wedding. I had never been so nervous to ask a question in my life! This felt like such a big question so soon! I looked down at the table and muttered an invite to be my plus-one:

> "So, I was invited to a wedding...in a month...in Chicago. I don't even know if you're single, but I really would love for you to come with me. Not as a friend, but as a date. Like a real date."

When I looked up, he was smiling back at me.

> "Yes! I'm single and I love weddings!"

WHAT?! I don't think I spoke for a few minutes after that response. This guy could indeed be the one! I felt a rush I had never felt before. It was amazing how much we had in common, like *a lot* in common! This was more than a crush. He might have reciprocal feelings for me and might even be the first to kiss me! We had a tentative date planned for a month out. In the meantime, I had no idea what to expect.

Two days later, I visited a friend to share the exciting news. I told her everything I liked about this guy and how excited I was for what was unfolding. The phone rang. It was him.

> "I think I told you about being a mentor for a high school robotics team. Well, our meeting ended early tonight, so I

wanted to know if you would like to go dancing at the bar tonight that you told me about, for an official first date?"

"Of course!"

"I'll pick you up in an hour?"

"Yes! I'm so excited!"

I had great anticipation as I had yet to be kissed, have a boyfriend, or even be on a date! My friend hurried to help me get ready so that I could feel and look my best.

I was living with my parents as I transitioned between graduate programs. So I was half-grateful and half-embarrassed to have my family present at the front door to send me off on my first date. I remember wearing my favorite purple summer dress that was fun to twirl in. He wore a handsome blue button-down shirt to dress up his jeans. He opened the car door for me and picked up the tab. If I was not already crazy about him, I was smitten when we danced cheek to cheek during our first dance.

He was a talented dancer and he taught me how to follow. I was accustomed to teaching a few steps to guys standing on the perimeter of the dance floor. Now, I had a guy leading me! He was *my* partner and I didn't have to share him the whole evening! Having watched *The Bachelor*, I felt as though this is how the girls felt when they had the bachelor all to themselves on a one-on-one date.

Nervous excitement and pure joy rushed through me all night. This man was everything I dreamed of and more. I felt safe in his arms and we were already taking pictures together. I love taking pictures and we were not wasting any time capturing these moments. That night on the dance floor was the catalyst for a month of memories together.

A week or so later, we went to an Indianapolis Indians baseball game and focused more on one another than the game on the field. The cleaning crew had to tell us that everybody had left the ballpark and they were locking up. He held my hand as we walked around downtown toward Monument Circle. It was an incredible feeling to experience the delight of holding hands with a man who was happy to be seen by my side. My feelings for him continued to develop as we shared our faith and prayed together for the first time on the steps of the monument in the heart of the city.

I saw him almost every day during that month and it is wild how close we felt in just a few weeks. At the beginning of the month, I did not even know if he was single. Now, after this life-changing month together, it felt natural to have him as my wedding date.

When he picked me up to head to the wedding, there was a certainty that I would remember this day forever. Since setting eyes on him for the first time, I had developed an image of who I thought he was. He took the opportunity in the car to share some of the reality of his life journey. He opened up in vulnerable ways that humbly reminded me of how the past can get in the way of the present. That day I not only chose him as a date, but also chose to love and accept him for who he truly was.

At the reception, my mind was still swirling with everything we had talked about on the road and the depth of our fast-growing friendship. My heart pumped with anxiety about the possibility of being kissed anytime now. After eating a delicious dinner, we walked together around the gorgeous, luxurious backyard. We discovered a life-size chess set and noticed people gathering around a fire pit. The sun had recently set and the lanterns on the trees lit up. I noticed he was leading me to a bench next to one of the decorated trees. It seemed as though I was in my own scene in a romantic comedy. As we sat down, I thought, how could the kiss not happen? Wait, I don't even know how to kiss! I cannot recall what we talked about, because I was just taking in the picturesque scene that surrounded us and waiting in anticipation for this long-awaited moment to happen. As I nuzzled under his arm, my anxious feelings calmed down a bit. I tried to savor every second of this feeling. It did not feel as though it could be real life. This guy was my date and he was here with me and for me.

After gazing happily into his eyes, I felt his lips on mine!

Ah! That was it! *My first kiss!* He kissed me!

He not only kissed me, but he helped boost my confidence since I was also no longer afraid of being a bad kisser. I hadn't had any practice, but I could not have asked for a more amazing first kiss!

As a dance instructor began teaching the wedding guests how to swing dance, I would normally be in a rush to be the first one on the floor. Today, I didn't want to be anywhere else than in his arms. Shortly after the kiss, he told me he wanted to introduce me to his family as his girlfriend at their 4th of July party the following week.

So, I had been kissed and entered into an exclusive relationship on the same night! What a rush this was!

The day was long. It was packed with emotion. Every muscle in my body was exhausted by the time we got to his car. I quickly fell asleep in the passenger seat as we drove to my friend's apartment in another suburb of Chicago. I was at peace waking up to him singing to his mixed CDs. He had a drawl in his voice and being personally serenaded was the cherry on top of this delicious day. I already felt so special and now I could completely relax with this guy and know that everything was going to be okay. I had found my match!

My exhaustion set in again as we figured out sleeping arrangements. I crossed off enough firsts in one day and this opportunity to share a bed did me in. I sat on the bathroom floor with my friend not knowing how to sleep in the same room with a guy who wasn't family. I had waited so long to cuddle with a man who reciprocated my feelings. An out-of-town wedding was not ideal for such an emotional day as this with a relationship so fresh. After taking some deep breaths, brushing my teeth, and telling him how nervous I was to share a bed, he assured me that there was no pressure or expectations for such an arrangement. I was calmed in his warm embrace and was relieved that we agreed to save sex for marriage. This guy was a keeper. I wanted to hold on to him forever and wanted to savor every minute we had together.

I was no longer single for the first time in my life and I could not be happier about the man who was by my side.

The years following that epic month would help me to understand the purpose of my long season of singleness. *I was waiting for this man to enter my life, and let me tell you, the wait was worth it!*

We often talked about our future together and we seemed inseparable. My close friends were married so they understood how I did not want to part from the love of my life at night. Though we abstained from sex and had different addresses, we often lived like a married couple. I started to recognize I was emotionally married to him without having a ring on my finger. I had nothing to worry about, because I knew we would be married eventually. Each year, we talked about an Easter wedding. I was excited for a church full of lilies in thanksgiving for St. Joseph bringing us together.

Soon after our first date, I moved into my grandparents' old house. He rented a house from my dad that was less than a mile away. It was convenient to be so close to one another and know I had a man committed to looking out for me. I wasn't used to that. I was also not used to having someone to cook with. We explored new recipes and took advantage of discounts on meal delivery kits. I couldn't get enough of his "Oh, hey, you!" greetings with his crooked smile at the front door, the times he got my jokes when others didn't, his shared tastes so we could split meals at restaurants, and his giddy excitement for adventures together. With him at 6 foot and me at 5 foot 9, bear hugs were perfect for him to kiss me on the forehead. As months and years passed by, those kisses on the forehead were priceless. Making out is of course a fun way to connect, but forehead kisses are so sweet and simple, and say so much.

Dancing together never lost its charm. We had a connection that none could match. Whether the dance floor was at a bar, at a wedding, on the street, or at home, it was ours for the taking. Multiple people approached us to say that we were going to make a great married couple.

When he was sent to the UK for a monthlong business trip, he paid for my flight to join him for a week. As a thank you, I packed our first Halloween costumes and surprised him with tickets to see *Mary Poppins* onstage! Yes, we were the only ones dressed as Mary and Bert in the audience, and we had a blast.

We were invited to represent Indianapolis at the World Meeting of Families in Philadelphia and were interviewed by international, national, and local news at the papal Mass. Hearing inspiring talks on marriage and seeing St. Gianna's wedding dress on display and meeting her daughter in person increased our desire even more to help one another become saints and to be a model married couple.

Everything checked out and our lives were pointing to marriage. My dad showed us some houses and we visited a friend's barn to consider the venue for our future wedding reception. We were invited to a dozen weddings and took notes after each. We were excited to throw the best party yet.

After our second anniversary, he began shopping for engagement rings as we talked about the future in greater detail. He was the first to come on a family vacation with me, and I traveled with his family as well. I was in family photos at each holiday gathering, and his family hinted that I would be his nephew's godmother. I was excited about becoming more and more a part of the family. The baptism arrived before I was ever asked. I learned that he was not ready to propose. We went to therapy for three months to work through some of the blocks that were keeping him from getting down on one knee after our fun, faith-filled relationship of two-and-a-half years.

After another Sunday of our leading small groups at RCIA (Rites of Christian Initiation for Adults), there was something that was off. He seemed avoidant and I was frustrated. He wasn't being as enthusiastic and cooperative as he had been. At my house afterward, he expressed the stress he was feeling over his life, his job, the ring shopping, the pressure, etc. He suggested that taking a break from the relationship for a month would probably help with the stress and possibly help clear his head. I had no idea how to respond to this. I felt paralyzed as I tried to process what was happening. We laid there for hours holding one another tight and sobbing. We both promised one another we would not hurt ourselves in our grief. He had experienced suicidal thoughts years before, and for the first time that evening I could begin to understand how people could become so hopeless. I could not fathom a world without him in it.

How could it help our lives for us to be apart? We were best friends and a team that adventured through life together. We had been talking about marriage since the beginning and I was confident that everything checked out. My world was crumbling before my eyes and we were talking about only taking a break for a month. I didn't have peace about this decision at all. Before him, my mom had been my confidant and the person I called about everything. Now, he had stepped into that role as we prepared for a lifetime together. Wasn't he my person? Who would I call now? Instead of attending a Super Bowl party together that night with family friends, *I was shocked that I was entering into a season of singleness once again.*

From being the big sister of quadruplet siblings to the third, fifth, or seventh wheel on group dates with friends, *I am familiar with the many ways that singleness feels.* Though I was single for most of my life, with the exception of my two-and-a-half-year relationship, *I was idolizing marriage and wasn't able to fully appreciate my current state in life.*

In this second season of singleness, I have become a stronger advocate for myself and others in this especially little-known season of life. My confusing and complicated breakup two years ago has prompted many women in similar situations to come to me with empathy and shared stories. My ears have been extra attentive to the lies that confuse singles and even those who search for their identity within relationships. *I've witnessed numerous interactions and participated in countless conversations about love in the counseling room, in the Church, and in my daily life.*

SINGLE TRUTH

I received the idea for this book as an answer to a prayer I offered on the way home from the final night of a parish mission in the fall of 2018. I was reminded to pray boldly to Our God. On that fall evening, I sat in the car on my driveway after arriving home from the parish mission and asked God what I can do during this season of fasting to bring Him glory. The answer was to write a book on what I have learned about love. *In this time of singleness, I have grown to experience love in a deeper way than ever before.* For two years following the confusing breakup, I asked God for the love of my life to have courage to choose love. My heart grew deeper *in love* rather than *out of love* throughout the process. It was clear that God was doing spiritual heart surgery on both of us in separate operating rooms. A couple of months before, I celebrated my 30th birthday by commencing a yearlong dating fast so that I could best cooperate with God in this healing process. For the record, this was definitely not the way I expected to celebrate this landmark in my life, and I have been faced with a great deal of misunderstanding and judgment from others who advise me that dating is the only way to heal.

Prior to the breakup, I was encouraged by many to write a book about our relationship. Our years together were full of surprises, fascinating details, funny stories, and answered prayers. I never guessed that I would finally get around to writing it two years after the shocking end. The plan was definitely not to write about the fruits of a breakup, *our* breakup. I still wrestle with this unanswered prayer.

Around the time I felt called to write this book, I was inspired by two authors I admire: Rebekah Lyons and Lysa TerKeurst. They both have written beautifully about anxiety and heartbreak. They are present to their readers as each authentically shares her heart on every page while admitting they don't have it all figured out. Though many authors write about something they've already processed, Rebekah shares her experience in her books as she's working through tough stuff herself. She writes that, *"Transparency is sharing where you've been, and vulnerability is sharing where you are."* The present can be raw and sometimes scary, but it is important to share. *"When you're alone and vulnerable, you feel afraid. When you're together and vulnerable, you become brave."*

As I read these words of hers about vulnerability especially and her struggle with anxiety, I was encouraged that I could be freed, too. Sharing our stories helps all involved. When we are in the middle of jumping a hurdle or processing a wound, we feel as if we are the only ones. That cannot be further from the truth, as shared suffering actually brings people together.

I have been moved by Lysa TerKeurst's humble humor, bold faith, and captivating witness to God walking with her through the unknown. She writes with an attitude of *"seeing blessings in the midst of things that look like burdens."* She calls out the hard realities of loneliness, isolation, confusion, and heartbreak by name. Our Lord provides for us, even when we don't understand.

Rebekah and Lysa are two beautiful women of faith who write from a perspective of a companion on the journey sitting down with you for coffee to swap stories and advice. This is how I hope this book is received. I am still working through these concepts and reflections each day and hope that these chapters can be just the beginning of deeper conversations in our families, churches, and communities. The process of writing itself has been an invitation to grow and expand in my understanding of God's presence in my story.

I have searched for a story worth telling because I love to write and share. The most transformational lesson in this season is that *I can find worth in my own story.* In a short amount of time, Bo Eason has taught me so much about storytelling and how others need to hear the stories we don't want to tell. He used to leave everything he had on the field when he played safety in the NFL. After retiring, he has taught people how to bring energy to the stage and bring their stories to life. People connect most authentically in real and raw moments.

During a few minutes I spent onstage with him, he began to peel back the layers of my own narrative I have told myself since childhood. More of the details will come later in this book, but I was humbly surprised to have that opportunity to declare in front of a theater of people that I matter.

There have been some beautiful ministries for those in the season of single life. Yet those leaders have reached their "happily ever after" and are encouraging the singles who are still waiting for that chapter of their lives to unfold.

I am convicted to write this book while I'm working through the truth about love while I'm still in the unknown as a single woman.

I, like you, don't know what is ahead in my story, but I do know that

God is the King of my heart and He helps me to experience wonder and awe in the waiting. He is teaching me how to be present to what He wants to show me now. My hope is that the pages ahead will help you see how God wants to show you His love in your life too—no matter what season you're in.

In everything, the Truth will set us free. Dancing around the subject or making assumptions doesn't help anyone. Jesus came to us as embodied Truth to accompany us and guide us along the paths that are polluted with lies. I have encountered so many lies that contaminate the hearts of souls that long for real love.

The title "Single Truth" came from time in prayer with God as I inquired about the fruit that could come from this season of diving into the love of Jesus and waiting to receive the love of a spouse. I felt as though the reason I was single was due to being overlooked or unwanted. Until I took an online course on loving the single life last year, I never fully embraced the advantages of being single. Instead, I was busy longing or even pining for a husband. The dictionary defines pining as "yearning deeply; suffering with longing; longing painfully."[1] Longing for a spouse is not all bad, but a spouse can never satisfy the longing in our hearts for God alone. St. Augustine's prayer declares, "O God! Our hearts are restless until we rest in You."

PEACE IN THE PRESENT

God alone is where our peace is found. God has brought you and me into the present moment exactly where He has called us to be at this time and place. To suffer with longing for any moment other than the one God has given us today can have implications in our relationship with God and with those we encounter today. At a recent Theology on Tap, Fr. Mike Schmitz posed a question to begin his talk:

"If you could be anywhere, where would you want to be?"

I found this question difficult to answer because I was joyfully content. I was currently sitting in the middle of a row of friends from my parish, on fire for the faith during a transformative conference, and was feet away from one of the most dynamic and entertaining

---

[1] https://www.dictionary.com/browse/pining

national Catholic speakers. I was so thrilled in the moment that it took a lot of work to think of anywhere else I would want to be. After people shouted out foreign cities across the world, their hometowns, or activities like taking a nap, Fr. Mike invited us to consider the joy of the present moment. He proceeded to speak about the power of living in the present. In therapy, we call this the here-and-now. It's not always what we would have expected or chosen if given the chance.

St. James challenges us to *"consider it all joy, my brothers, when you encounter various trials."*[2] A homily recently highlighted the word *consider* in this verse. The joy in the moment will not always be obvious, but we can be aware of God's promises and think about the grace in the moment. Let us keep one another accountable to make our requests be known to God and wait on Him actively by living our lives with a trusting heart rather than with painful discontent.

In this book, I hope my personal reflections encourage you as a single person yourself or help you to reevaluate your perspective of love in your life and relationships. Marriage in the Church is an image of God's love for His people. The couple enters a covenant of love that is free, faithful, and fruitful. This love is not exclusively for married couples, but rather demonstrated for the world through a marital covenant. As I laid out my chapters, I was tickled to find that the themes described how one can give and receive a love that is free, faithful, and fruitful even in a season of singleness.

Lysa TerKeurst explained how God asked her to write a book last year that she would need to read this year. I know, for myself, I am being asked to write this book now so that I can read it later when I become forgetful of the lessons and overwhelmed in the busy-ness of marriage and family. There's something about hitting rock bottom or being without that gives God the space to come and restore. When we're on the mountaintop, we need to be reminded of what we learned in the valley.

SINGLE MARRIAGE COUNSELOR

Through my pursuit of a marriage and family counseling license, I have heard the following questions multiple times:

---

[2] James 1:2 (NABRE)

12

"What do you know about love?"

"Why would anyone come to you for marriage advice if you're not married yourself?"

Though I fought these questions before ever having a significant other, I was hopeful that a man in shining armor would help me to put those questions to rest. Five years after graduating with my degree in marriage counseling, I am still single. It was especially difficult after the breakup to reason with God about how the clients in front of me, who did not talk or pray together, were still together as a couple, while my love and I were not—even though many told us that we as a couple modeled all the right practices in the way we loved talking and praying together. It has been humbling to know I don't have to understand it. I just have to accept it.

Through this season, I have been invited to dive deeper into my professional life and reflect on my capacity to love and be loved. Throughout the aftermath of my breakup, I have heard poor and potentially harmful pieces of advice and ideas of love. I feel called to share what I have learned about love from the perspective as a single marriage counselor and as a faith-filled single woman in my 30s. My heart, like those of clients who sit across from me on the couch, is wounded and looks for true love not to eradicate the wounds, but to mercifully shine light through the cracks.

My favorite definition of mercy is "love touching misery." I want to apply that to an image presented to me the day I graduated from Saint Mary's College.

Ring the bells that still can ring. Forget your perfect offering.
There is a crack in everything—that's how the light gets in.[3]

I invite you to keep these words in mind as you journey with me through this book. I pray that my authentic offering in this season of discovery touches your heart in a new way.

---

[3] Saint Mary's College 2011 Commencement Address referencing Leonard Cohen's "Anthem" lyrics

I

Love Is Free:
You Are Worthy of Love

1

CHECKLIST BEFORE CHECKMATE:
LOVE IS NOT A REWARD

"Trust in the Lord and do good; live in the land and be safe. Seek your happiness in the Lord, and he will give you your heart's desire. Give yourself to the Lord; trust in Him, and He will help you... Be patient and wait for the Lord to act... Don't give in to worry or anger."[4]

I invite you to take out a blank piece of paper. It may be one of the last pages of a cherished journal or a random notepad on the kitchen counter. Jot down a list of qualities you hope to find in a spouse. What really matters to you? This list is not a list of groceries, but rather ingredients for a relationship. It's a way to express your heart's request on paper.

"What are you looking for?"[5]

Jesus posed this question to His early disciples, and He asks us the same question today as we follow Him. What happens inside you as He asks *you*? What are *you* looking for?

Have you ever asked a concierge at a hotel or a local on a street corner for directions? If you do not know where you want to go, the directions will not be much help. Rather, if you spend some time thinking about how you want to spend your time and sites you would like to see, directions will provide you with direct steps to accomplish your vision. It is helpful to make a list of qualities you hope to see in

---

[4] Psalm 37:3-5, 7, 8 (GNT)
[5] John 1:38 (NABRE)

a spouse because ultimately it reflects the type of person *you* want to be. It helps you focus on the qualities *you* want to have with and within you.

DISTINCT

I often describe myself as ambitious. I want to be more and do more. I want to stand out. I want to be special and distinct. These earnest desires were certainly sparked through wrestling with my identity as a big sister of quadruplets.

For two-and-a-half years, I had undivided attention as an only child as Mom and Dad fought for their turn to hold me. My parents then brought home four younger siblings who shared pretty much everything, including a birthday. Visitors to our home were happily handed a baby and a bottle to be productive during their stay. Overnight, there were more children than parents. My world was rocked and quickly I began to explore what made me distinct as a non-quad.

If I was not distinct, I would be overlooked.

That became a deep fear within me for decades.

I held tight to my distinct role as the big sister. I wanted to be the best big sister I could be. I wanted to experience everything first. It was a unique role that only I could have in the family. I found my distinction as a role model and trial kid.

I paved the way for my siblings through sports and extracurricular activities by providing feedback for them as they followed the trail I blazed. For example, I was a cheerleader in 4th grade. Though I thoroughly enjoyed borrowing my mom's sunglasses for a 4th-grade-football halftime parody performance of "We are the Men in Black" ("We are SPX"), the cheerleading practices conflicted with volleyball practices. Since volleyball brought me more joy, cheerleading was the first thing to get removed from my schedule. My little sisters therefore never had their turn at cheering, "Defense, defense, take that ball away!"

I especially remember feeling overlooked when my siblings and I participated in an NSYNC contest on the radio. The five of us could represent each member of the band. We went all out and dressed like the picture on their premiere album, in basketball jerseys and tear-away pants. I know…we were too cool for school. We sang and danced for the deejays even though listeners obviously couldn't see us. When our creative band name The Quads Plus One was announced, the emcee forgot to say, "plus one." Even though I know that I was not intentionally forgotten, I remember how much it hurt. I was just one and I wanted to count. I wanted to be seen, heard, and noticed for who I was rather than getting lost in the mix.

Though my goals to lead well and become an excellent example to my siblings are good, it has also been exhausting as I have leaned on an identity I have falsely assumed rather than the one God has truly given me. Rather than trying to maintain control over this identity, I have been invited to humbly accept my role as a sister among them more than a sister above them. As they often remind me, we're actually only two years apart. We all frequently compete for attention. Come hang out with my family any day and you will be greeted by a loud bunch with lots of love and short attention spans. In a busy house, we might have all been seeking to externally process and relate to the others. Even in the chaos, my family loved me and accepted me for who I was and they still do today.

During my season as a single woman, I have not had a partner to romance me, but I have had many loved ones to accompany me.

FREE TO BE

As I wait for friendship to develop into a partnership for life, I am humbly reminded that I cannot control who others are or what they do. I am encouraged that I *can* control who I am and what I do. When we are looking for friends, we can work on being the type of friend we want to find. When we are hoping a friend or partner can improve in a particular area, we can model for them by improving ourselves in that area first.

We can tell God what we desire and then we can reflect and see whether we can recognize those qualities in ourselves. We then are invited to pray and surrender to God, knowing He will provide the grace to help us and give us every good and perfect gift in perfect timing.

Prayer doesn't change God; it changes us. As we make our intentions known, we can direct our hearts toward heaven. We are the ones who can make the space by decluttering that which distracts and standing ready to be filled with that which satisfies our souls.

Jesus asks, *"What can I do for you?"*

What is on your to-do list? Where do you want to see God act in your life? He wants to satisfy the innermost part of our hearts. He has the world in His hands and reveals His radiance in the sunrise and sunset every single day.

God told St. Teresa of Avila, "I would create the world again just to hear you say, 'I love you.'" God loves us because He created us. And He didn't need to create us. He wanted to create you and me because He wants to be loved by His creation. Since He *is* love, He understands that love is free. We cannot earn His love, and the crucifixion proved that He can't earn ours. Regardless of the boxes checked and acts done, He is there with open arms. There is nothing I can do to make God love me more, and there is nothing I can do to make God love me less.

ENOUGH

Family and friends affirm me in my physical appearance and personality and then sometimes inquire why I am still single. They may say, "You are so beautiful and fun; why aren't you dating?" or, "If you're still single, God must be trying to teach you something before you're ready to meet someone." Though these are said with good intentions, they connote a lack or fault in one's worth if their relationship status is single. Just typing out these phrases brings up feelings of exhaustion and inadequacy as others suggest I must not be open *enough* or trying hard *enough* to find someone. I must still have more work to do.

A romantic relationship, or any loving relationship for that matter, is a gift, not a reward. It doesn't follow a checklist or have a cause-and-effect correlation. Christ's gifts are not ours because we earned them, but because we inherit them through His name. Love is not a reward and is not something we need to be afraid to lose. St. Paul writes to the Romans about not being afraid because we are adopted sons and daughters of God:

> *For those who are led by the Spirit of God are children of God. For you did not receive a spirit of slavery to fall back into fear, but you received a spirit of adoption, through which we cry, "Abba, Father!"*[6]

For the Romans, parents were able to abandon their children after birth if they were not what they wanted. But adoptive parents knew what they were getting and therefore entered into an unbreakable

---

[6] Romans 8:14-15 (NABRE)

bond with their new child. The child became a new person in that his or her name was changed, and any debts were forgiven. The child was accepted as a biological child and shared adoptive parents' rights and inheritances.

Our adoptive father is love Himself and He "proves his love for us in that while we were still sinners Christ died for us."[7] He neither came nor died for us because we deserved Him, but because His hour had come to wed His bride. He claims us as His own. He knows exactly what He's doing. He is never late. We are not powerful enough to hinder His plan. "For as the heavens are higher than the earth, so are my ways higher than your ways, my thoughts higher than your thoughts."[8]

Satan is sneaky though and flirts with our desire to control. In the Garden of Eden, the serpent's lie was the same as it is today. He whispers, "God is holding out on you." He tells us that if God loved us, we could eat and have whatever we wanted. I have been like Eve, who let the serpent convince her she needed to grasp for her identity in earthly attachments. I am becoming more like Mary, who allowed Christ to work through her as an instrument that is full of grace and trust. God has provided all the grace I need for this moment and the next. All I am called to do is open my hands and receive God's goodness.

CHECKMATE ON OUR HEARTS

God knows us better than we know ourselves and chooses to love us unconditionally. As human beings, there is nothing we can do to earn that divine love He offers to us so freely. In the Roman Catholic liturgy, we exclaim, "We are not worthy that You should enter under our roof."

Minutes after this, God graciously offers His only Son's Body, Blood, Soul, and Divinity in the Eucharistic bread. *He models for us that "yes" is a gift and not an obligation. When we go through this life striving to earn or deserve the reward of relationship, we are missing out on the gift that a relationship truly is.* When a couple comes to my office in discord, I ask them to tell me the story of how they met and fell in love. Their eyes gloss over with wonder and awe. They stop fighting for a time as they remember the gift that they have received in the partner God

---

7 Romans 5:8 (NABRE)
8 Isaiah 55:9 (NABRE)

has brought them.

As you wait in this season, do you pray about what is to come more than you worry about it? I'm guilty of worrying before praying. I admittedly complain to God or become paralyzed in my lack rather than letting God know what's in my heart. When we go to God with requests, we are asked to come with gratitude for the countless gifts we have already been given. It's with a grateful heart that we can truly see that God has already called "checkmate" on our souls and in our lives. We cannot compete with that.

Reflection: In what areas or ways do you feel entitled to love rather than receiving what God brings?

2

FREE TO GIVE ALL

"How I love your Temple, Lord Almighty! How I want to be there! I long to be in the Lord's temple. With my whole being I sing for joy to the living God... How happy are those who live in your Temple, always singing praise to you... One day spent in your Temple is better than a thousand anywhere else."[9]

There is a place in my heart for the Mardi Gras season, New Orleans culture, and Cajun cuisine. My parents went to New Orleans for an MLK date weekend a few times when my siblings and I were growing up. They brought home authentic beads and festive masks that were fun to wear on out-of-uniform days at school and to add to spirit wear when we were cheering on our favorite teams. I have developed a fondness for the food and the culture that only reached new heights after I visited New Orleans during Mardi Gras season. I am a Hoosier through and through, but I enjoy bringing some Cajun joy to my friends in Indiana who don't yet share my appreciation.

In this second season of singleness, I have hosted an annual party at my house on Mardi Gras. This year, I spent the afternoon cooking six different authentic dishes, and I was eager to introduce each one to my guests. I have little experience and creativity in the

---

[9] Psalm 84:1-2, 4, 10 (GNB)

kitchen, but hosted an authentic party with non-processed, delicious food I was proud of! Cooking for one can be uneventful, so having a house full of people to feed was a refreshing and exhilarating challenge. I am inspired to take advantage of my time and energy in this season to reach out and initiate invitations rather than simply waiting for others to invite me first.

EMPTINESS AS WHOLENESS

As a single person, I feel as though my relationship status is associated with a half-glass-empty image. Single life is often viewed as being without or being unfulfilled. I can be distracted by the lack of a partner to love me, rather than focusing attention on the abundance of opportunities to love others. Time, especially for women, can seem to be running out, and they can often take the attitude that if a partner does not miraculously appear soon, they will become depleted of hope and doomed to a life of singleness forever with no husband and no kids. Dramatic, I know, but not far from the theme of some interactions I've witnessed. As I've gained a new perspective on this season of life, I have learned that it can indeed be viewed as full, rather than empty.

To live wholeheartedly is to be "fully or completely sincere, enthusiastic, energetic, hearty, or earnest."[10] This fullness is not about what is received from the outside, but rather what is given from the inside. From a single perspective, it is easy to think that our hearts can't be full without love from a partner. However, living a wholehearted life is an offering that can be made in every season.

Though we cannot control others or circumstances we encounter, we can discern how to best respond and live each day. Being wholehearted is to live boldly. Living boldly does not require clenched fists. Exhaustion and worry actually lead to a lack of flexibility, whereas enthusiasm can bring joy and an open mind.

An image of prayer that intrigues me is open hands. When you pick up a handful of sand and tighten your grasp, grains spill out like a waterfall. Cupping sand with open hands with palms facing up allows for some sand to go and some to stay. By the same token, when I have my hands completely full of groceries or other items when entering a building, it's nearly impossible to open the door for someone else. I have to drop something to be available to welcome

---

others. In my season now, I can answer the call of friends and family with an open, ready, and accessible heart. When I want to either attend or host an event, I can proceed without asking permission. One of the most radically beautiful aspects of relationships is loving God through the accountability of a spouse. Without a partner, I am invited to give my whole heart to God in a way that people in relationships do not.

FREE OF DISTRACTIONS

St. Paul, in his letter to the Corinthians, advocates for sacred single life:

> I should like you to be free of anxieties. An unmarried man is anxious about the things of the Lord, how he may please the Lord. But a married man is anxious about the things of the world, how he may please his wife, and he is divided. An unmarried woman or a virgin is anxious about the things of the Lord, so that she may be holy in both body and spirit. A married woman, on the other hand, is anxious about the things of the world, how she may please her husband. I am telling you this for your own benefit, not to impose a restraint upon you, but for the sake of propriety and adherence to the Lord without distraction.[11]

A quote that can paraphrase St. Paul's message is, "It's better to be single and wanting to be married than to be married and wanting to be single." As a single person, you have many opportunities to serve God and others. The desire for marriage is good and healthy, but if you're thinking that your life is contingent on attaining that relationship status, you will miss the benefits of single life. For St. Paul, there were clearly many benefits to the freedom of singleness. Married life brings a different sort of freedom in that you no longer have to search or wonder about who your future spouse will be. You are free to choose to simply love that person every day.

Gatherings like my Mardi Gras party didn't require me to be married or even in a romantic relationship. In this season, I have a schedule that allows me to cook in the afternoon, a house with a couple of tables and chairs, and a heart that is eager to share my enthusiasm about life. There is no need to wait for a partner to fill

---

[11] 1 Cor 7:32-35 (NABRE)

your heart. Our dependence on others to determine the capacity of our hearts to give and to receive can be troublesome. It can produce emotional clutter in our lives that can distract us from the simple truth that God is declaring over our hearts. *There is a place in His heart that only we can fill, and there's a place in our hearts that only He can fill.*

One of the greatest blessings in prayer during this season is filling my heart with God's love by prioritizing Mass and Adoration in my daily schedule. It is amazing to witness the power of managing my time before it manages me. During a short exchange with a friend a few years ago, I expressed sadness at not having time to read. She told me that I did indeed have time; I just didn't use it for reading. Everything that is on my calendar is mainly there because I allowed it to be there. Think about that for a minute. Everything in your schedule was in some way permitted by you to be there. As employees, we agree to certain precedents about meetings and requirements. We spend our time off of work doing something, but typically not what edifies us most or brings us true rest and relaxation. We are not always sure who is in control between ourselves and our schedules.

Without a housemate to check in with before or after work besides my sweet kitty, Magdalene, I have chosen to fill that chunk of the relational part in my heart with God. In my present situation, I am invited to totally depend on God for direction, comfort, and refuge in the storms of the unknown. I am open and available to spend this special time with Him without kids or a spouse needing my attention. This time has become a cherished gift that I know I will miss once I enter a new season.

DECLUTTERED

My phenomenal counselor has invited me during this season to declutter my identity as I am able to fully reflect on how I can step into my best self before a family's opinion may confuse me. When I was so deeply in love with a partner, I allowed others more permission to influence my current and future self. On my own, now, I am free to get a clearer picture of that for myself before welcoming a spouse and in-laws.

Simplifying and decluttering spaces in our lives are also new mainstream practices that people are taking on. Marie Kondo's show on Netflix leads many viewers to investigate their own closets and see how many bags of stuff they can remove from their spaces. The removal of the unnecessary provides a space to honor what is best, favored, and necessary. Living currently in my grandparents' former home, I'm still experiencing the weight of decluttering belongings that Beebah and Peepah left behind when they passed away.

It's more stressful to have to filter through each article of clothing in a full closet than it is to have a less cluttered closet with space for a new gift. When we are open and excited for what God will bring in a future spouse, we are in a much better position for prayer than if we are weighed down and stuck in a lifelong relationship that we no longer desire. *If God satisfies our hearts and makes them whole, why do we approach the throne with a mind-set that we are lacking anything?* We can generate positive or negative energy in what we think and do. *When I am free of unnecessary attachments, my yoke is lighter, my head is clearer, and I discover energy that helps me serve others.* God's grace is abundant and is there for you and me right now.

Reflection: How can you declutter your heart so it can be filled with love?

3

GOD IS LOVE AND YOU ARE LOVED

"Give thanks to the Lord, because he is good; his love is eternal... He alone performs great miracles; his love is eternal. By his wisdom he made the heavens; his love is eternal; he built the earth on the deep waters; his love is eternal. He made the sun and the moon; his love is eternal; the sun to rule over the day; his love is eternal; the moon and the stars to rule over the night; his love is eternal."[12]

My parents were the first to teach me about love. They were married in 1985 when "The Power of Love" was number one on the charts. They are best friends, go on dates every weekend, and regularly hang out with the same group of loyal friends they have known since before they were married. From their loving marriage of committed friendship, I was born into the world.

When I was two years old, my world was turned on its head. I was an only child who was never short of any love or attention who was now watching my mom's belly grow larger and larger. In March of 1991, I was excited to go stay at Beebah and Peepah's house (I am grateful to actually live in this same house today). They lived in Christian Park and met their neighbors each morning for a walk in the park. Beebah snacked on graham crackers spread with jelly, and Peepah napped through soap operas. After delicious homemade dinners, we walked across the bridge to Dairy Queen for ice-cream cones.

---

[12] Psalm 136:1-9 (GNT)

I can only guess that to me as a two-year-old, this visit seemed normal. My life when I returned home would be anything but ordinary. One by one, my new quadruplet siblings were introduced to me. I petted them gently as though they were puppies and then recognized the reality that they would be playmates! What an incredible blessing they were. I would never be alone again and would always have someone to play with.

Reporters from the local news came to spend the night with our family to see what life was like with quadruplets. As I look back on videos of that TV special, I notice that I am squeezed in the middle of the couch shoulder to shoulder with our new family of seven. Though my birth was a miracle from the perspective of my parents who struggled with infertility, it wasn't newsworthy like having four babies at once. Being a big sister of quadruplets became my most prominent fun fact and the source of my pride and joy. I was not a quad, but I was a BIG sister!

Ever since those cameras came to our home and the interest revolved around the quads, I have been afraid of being forgotten. Not neglected, not unloved; just an afterthought in the shadow of my little brothers and sisters. The role I took on in the family was the entertainer and the protector. I soaked up any attention to the point of being obnoxious in home videos, repeatedly saying things like, "Mom, watch this," or, "Mom, look at me." I strived to be a role model, the star, and the best big sister. I was a little confused to hear my parents tell me to just be a sister and not work so hard on standing out.

I am grateful that my parents helped me to understand God's devoted, unconditional love for me by never wavering in their love for the five of us.

LOVE

I often exclaim, "I love love!" Beyond family life, love has captured me in many ways from childhood to present day. I developed strong crushes on celebrities and peers, watched romantic comedies, grew up in a close and loyal family, and pursued degrees in counseling and theology. I've been fascinated by why we do what we do or believe what we believe. My aspiration to be a counselor is rooted in helping other families find the love I experienced in my own home.

In a beautiful homily about love, a priest stated, "Love requires the surrender of one's life." Having my world bombarded with four siblings at the same time was both the greatest blessing and the biggest challenge I have faced. I work weekly with a therapist to process the implications of my identity and this tremendous transition at such a young age. One of the definitions of *surrender* is "to yield or resign in favor of another."[13] I've resisted any resignation because I was afraid of losing myself in the process. Now, I have learned it's not about losing oneself, but giving oneself in love. St. Gianna said, "Love and sacrifice are clearly linked, like the sun and the light. We cannot love without suffering and we cannot suffer without love."

Love and suffering are actually the only two guarantees in life. God created each human being by love, in love, and for love. In this fallen world, however, we experience sin and suffering. We haven't arrived at our eternal home so there will be suffering along the way. Mother Teresa beautifully described suffering as "a kiss from Christ on the cross."

The cross reminds us that Our Lord was crucified for a crime He never committed and suffered a death He never deserved. Yet He laid down His life for us to model that "the greatest love is to lay down one's life for another." Good Friday is good because it's the most radical love that God modeled for us.

Spoiler alert: love didn't stay on the cross.

Love yielded to the cross and made space for the glory of the resurrection. Love begets love. As we surrender ourselves for others, we feel loved, too. One of the most beautiful examples of this surrender is Mary, the Mother of Jesus. When the angel Gabriel came to surprise her with news that she—a virgin—would give birth to the Savior of the World, she was troubled because she did not understand. Gabriel assured her that nothing is impossible with God.[14] Her deep love for God was expressed in her fiat, "Behold, I am the handmaid of the Lord. May it be done to me according to your word."[15]

Though many readers may interpret handmaid as a slave of some kind, a more accurate translation would compare the

---

[13] https://www.dictionary.com/browse/surrender
[14] Luke 1:37 (NABRE)
[15] Luke 1:38 (NABRE)

relationship to the way lovers serve one another. Lovers are not ordered by a power-hungry master, but rather delighted to make the other their first priority. When two people fall in love, the beloved seems to receive all of one's focus and attention. All he wants is what she wants, and all she wants to know is what he knows. Time spent together is never long enough and they happily go out of their way to help one another. Mary's fiat is a model for us to know that the more we know and love God, the more natural it is to serve Him. Her grown son, Jesus, proclaimed, "I no longer call you slaves, because a slave does not know what his master is doing. I have called you friends, because I have told you everything I have heard from my Father."[16] Jesus is our friend and He wants to share everything with us. If you have been in any sort of relationship, you know that *everything* includes the good, bad, and the ugly.

THANKFUL FOR THE CROSS

After spending a couple of hours writing this book in a fancy hotel lobby, I took a break and walked down the street to my beautiful downtown parish for daily Mass. I examined my mind and heart for what to offer up on this day. I wasn't alone long before my ex genuflected and entered the opposite side of my pew. We exchanged smiles and nods but kept our distance by a few feet. Sharing a sign of peace through a handshake helped me to reconcile without words. Being so close to, and yet so far from, someone I love dearly challenged my heart and deepened my understanding of God's love. On the drive home, I heard myself utter the words,

"Lord, thank you for this cross because it helps me depend on you.

"Thank you for this cross because it helps me know how much you love me.

"Thank you for this cross because through it I can actually love him more!"

Wow. When our hearts ache for someone and the feelings are not reciprocated, or the timing is not right, we can learn more about how God loves us. God radically pursues and proves His love and faithfulness in every word and deed. He's madly in love with you and eagerly waits for you to love Him in return.

---

[16] John 15:15 (NABRE)

In this life, the cross can either stand as a barrier as our sinfulness leads us away from the divine romance we are called to or it can be a highway on a path to true love. Fulton Sheen argues that "some will not look on suffering because it creates responsibility." While Jesus was carrying the cross to Calvary, a man named Simon of Cyrene was pulled from the crowd and asked to help Jesus carry His cross. He had already fallen and still had a long way to go to His destination. At that point of encounter, Simon was invited to take responsibility in order to carry the cross. This was not on his to-do list for the day, and it was surely humiliating to be in the limelight in the chaotic scene. Even if Simon was pushed or persuaded, he took the step to accompany Jesus by helping with the load on His shoulders. In joining in the suffering, Simon was intimately closer to Christ than the by-standing crowd. This illustrates Sheen's insight that "it's only through suffering that we can be truly one with Jesus on this side of Heaven."

The cross is not meant to be carried alone, and our Father knows our littleness better than we do. St. Therese saw the stairway to sainthood as too intimidating for a childlike heart to climb. She wanted to find an elevator to escalate the climb. She suggested that if we accept that littleness and ask for help, He will gladly take us into His arms and lift us up to Himself. Pride unfortunately often keeps us from asking to be carried. In our personal stories, it often takes hitting rock bottom to recognize that we cannot do it on our own. God allows that experience to save us as we remember to depend on Him through everything.

FREE TO KNOW

"God is love"[17] and He teaches us that love is free. God is free to love in His own way. Through Adam and Eve, He gave you and me free will to choose Him and love in our own way. He willed human beings into existence that were in His image but were not Him. He thus allows us to have our own space for discovering who we are and who we are becoming. Parents model this free expression of love when they give their children space to explore. This does not mean hands-off. Love is not coercive, but it can be convicting. God invites and pursues us daily, but we can choose whether we want to

---

[17] 1 John 4:8 (NLT)

receive that love. From the cross in the ultimate act of love, Jesus exclaimed, "I thirst!" He wants us to thirst for His love and ask to be filled up.

We ask to be filled up through communicating with Him throughout our day in prayer. St. Therese's understanding of prayer is "a surge of the heart; it is a simple look turned toward heaven; it is a cry of recognition and of love, embracing both trial and joy." St. Teresa of Calcutta spent her prayer time "looking at God and God looking back at her." She explained that "prayer begins with you beholding God as He beholds you."

Isn't it true that kids feel loved by those who waste time with them? When you waste time with someone, you are letting them know that there is no place you'd rather be. God the Father likes to waste time with us too. When was the last time you spent time with Him?

One of the ways to practice this is through Eucharistic Adoration. Since Catholics believe that the substance of the bread and wine in Church transforms into the Body and Blood of Christ, we have the opportunity to look at God in a real, mysterious way through a monstrance. This practice "demonstrates" God's humble, loving gaze for all those who draw near to Him and visit. Fulton Sheen said, "The greatest love story of all time is contained in a tiny white host."

When Moses asked to know God's name, He said, "I AM." He is God and we are not. He can handle the throne and doesn't need to be told how to be himself. He IS love. Not all experiences in our lives will feel loving from our perspective, but God asks us to trust His sovereignty and providence as He wills all things for good for those who love Him in return.

I think of the story about the human father not giving his son a snake if he asks for a fish.[18] How much more would our Father in heaven, who is perfect, give us?! What a good Father we have! We come to know and love our Father through prayer. Prayer doesn't just help our relationship, it *is* our relationship. God is the essence of being. We cannot move or breathe without God willing each and every moment for us. The fact that you are reading this right now means that you are alive—life is flowing through you! It is God's will that you are existing today! As He was creating the world, He knew

---

[18] Luke 11:5-13 (NABRE)

that the world would not be the same without you.

LOVE IS VISIBLE

We learn in the story of creation that Adam and Eve were made in the image and likeness of God. We are called human *beings.* So, if God is love, we are made from, in, and for love! St. Pope John Paul the Great has written inexhaustibly on how our bodies have been created for love. These writings have been compiled as the Theology of the Body. Christopher West and Jason Evert are two prolific writers who have helped translate this wisdom for the modern day. These men vulnerably share their own experiences and insights into the profound teachings of our late Holy Father. St. John Paul II said, "The body, and it alone, is capable of making visible what is invisible: the spiritual and the divine. It was created to transfer into the visible reality of the world the mystery hidden since time immemorial in God [God's love for man], and thus to be a sign of it."[19]

I want to emphasize that God did not want us to be forced to love Him but to be pursued in love. How romantic and mysterious! "God places such a high premium on our freedom that he shies away from forcing us to do things that would benefit us. He understands that we will never learn to love or respond to him without that costly freedom."[20] He gives us freedom to be and love in our own way. After reading Henry Cloud's writing on God's boundaries, I began making more of an effort to let God be God and love me the way He wants to.

"Freedom exists for the sake of love."[21] In our relationships on earth, we don't want our loved ones to love us solely out of obligation. Providing a healthy space to choose one another freely day after day draws us deeper in relationship. It is also this freedom that causes pain. Those you love most will hurt you most. We are imperfect and weak.

St. Paul invites us to not run from our weaknesses, because "[God's] power is made perfect in weakness." We know that God uses our weaknesses for His glory. There is nothing God does not use for our good. "That is why, for Christ's sake, I delight in weaknesses, in insults, in hardships, in persecutions, in difficulties.

---

[19] St. John Paul the Great, "Theology of the Body," February 20, 1980
[20] Henry Cloud, *Boundaries in Marriage*
[21] St. John Paul the Great, *Love and Responsibility*

For when I am weak, then I am strong."[22] It's always a win-win with God. We are simply asked to return to Him again and again. The law of the gift is that "the more we give to Him, the more gifts we receive as our offerings are transformed."

When I work with couples, I remind them that no one ever said love—most certainly not marriage—is easy. No one…ever. In fact, Jesus says, "There is no greater love than to lay down one's life for a friend." The passionate love of God was illustrated in Jesus' carrying of the cross. If we truly believe that everything in this life happens for our salvation, our eyes turn to heaven and see how God is forming us as loving disciples. When asking us to follow Him, our Lover tells us to "pick up our crosses." So, love was never promised to be an easy journey. However, without the Resurrection, there is no cross. Without the Cross, there is no resurrection. So, it is the carrying of our daily crosses in life that conforms us to the love of God and teaches us how to love like He does.

St. Paul encourages us, "Do not grow slack in zeal, be fervent in spirit, serve the Lord. Rejoice in hope, endure in affliction, persevere in prayer."[23]

We love what we know. At Calvary, we killed what we didn't know. We didn't know how to accept the depth of love that gazed at us from eyes that know us more intimately than we know ourselves. The crucifixion and death of Our Lord illustrate the reckless and incomprehensible love of God. At the same time, we remember how difficult it is to accept such unconditional love. The night before my friend's wedding, her groom shared with me that he still felt inadequate and unlovable. My friend's love for him was very deep and he did not understand how he could be worthy of such fervent love. Though he didn't always see his own worthiness, he took her as his bride, and they are beautiful witnesses to marriage today.

FEARLESS

"There is no fear in love, but perfect love drives out fear because fear has to do with punishment, and so one who fears is not yet perfect in love."[24] St. John Paul the Great, in his inaugural homily

---

22 2 Corinthians 12:9-10 (NIV)
23 Romans 12:11-12 (NABRE)
24 1 John 4:18 (NABRE)

when he became pope, said,

> Do not be afraid to welcome Christ and accept his power… Do not be afraid. Open wide the doors for Christ… Do not be afraid. Christ knows 'what is in man.' He alone knows it. So often today man does not know what is within him, in the depths of his mind and heart. So often he is uncertain about the meaning of his life on this earth. He is assailed by doubt, a doubt which turns into despair. We ask you therefore, we beg you with humility and trust, let Christ speak to man. He alone has words of life, yes, of eternal life.[25]

Let us not be afraid to love and be loved. In Scripture, the command *"Do not be afraid"* actually appears 365 times! So, there is never a day that we are off the hook. In the counseling room, fear is usually the catalyst for regret.

Fear keeps us from taking that chance.

Fear keeps us from communicating our true feelings.

Fear keeps us from experiencing true love.

You do not have to be overcome with fear, because Jesus is here.

Reflection: What has your experience taught you about love?

---

[25] St. John Paul the Great, "Homily for the Inauguration of His Pontificate" October 22, 1978

II

Love Is Faithful:
Your Feelings Are Valid

4

SILENCE: LISTENING TO THE LOVER

"How clearly the sky reveals God's glory! How plainly it shows what he has done! Each day announces it to the following day; each night repeats it to the next. No speech or words are used, no sound is heard; yet their message goes out to all the world and is heard to the ends of the earth. God made a home in the sky for the sun; it comes out in the morning like a happy bridegroom, like an athlete eager to run a race."[26]

As I start this chapter on silence, I imagine you and I looking at one another without saying anything. But, since this is a book, a blank chapter would not be too useful. I should probably write something to help guide us as I type in silence and you read in silence. I do invite you to close your eyes for a minute and take three deep breaths. What do you hear around you? How do you feel when you're silent? Relieved? Resistant? Restful?

Walking the Camino de Santiago in the Summer of 2018, I experienced the beauty of silence. I was traveling across the pond by myself, so I brought headphones in case I wanted to listen to an audio book or music during the long days of hiking. Pilgrims from all over the world and various states in life travel along the Camino to delve into the silence rather than detract from it. When I wasn't sharing in conversation along the Way, I savored the silence. Whether the Spanish landscape was rural or urban, wet or sunny, the sweetness of silence could be found.

---

[26] Psalm 19:1-5 (GNT)

ACTIVE LISTENING

As a counselor, I have been taught to be comfortable with silence to provide space for clients to process their thoughts and reply when they are ready. If I refrain from speaking for a few minutes, my clients will eventually break the ice and go into more detail. The point of the session, after all, is to hear the clients express what they are working through. My main goal as a marriage counselor is to express empathy to clients and model active listening skills. When a couple comes to meet with me in session, each partner is trying to communicate a message to the other. However, that message is not getting through effectively. This is either because of the way it's being delivered or because the other person is focused on their own perspective, hindering them from actually listening.

In session, I typically invite one partner to turn to the other and share what they need from them. More often than not, the receiver is immediately defensive. I stop the receiver in their tracks and invite them to first repeat verbatim what they heard. This seemingly elementary task takes many tries. It seems impossible for them to simply repeat what they heard, let alone without any personal commentary along with it.

This daily experience in the therapy room transfers to struggles with prayer. *If it is difficult to sit face-to-face with someone and listen with our ears, then it is obviously going to take time to learn how to sit in Jesus' presence and listen with our hearts.* Distractions in both scenarios are similar as we worry about to-do lists and our own understanding and perspectives.

From the therapy chair, I get a glimpse of what God sees when He watches us struggle to connect. We beg for God to give us answers, but we keep reaching for everything except the answer. Ultimately, Jesus is the answer. An old Sunday school joke suggests that when you don't know the answer, say, "Jesus." Though it seems as if it's cheating to repeat the same answer over and over again, Jesus is indeed the answer. There's actually power in simply saying His name!

Speaking has power in itself. God could have created in any way He wanted, and He chose to speak life into existence. He said, "Let there be light," and there was light. In this past year, I have worked with Roger Love, who is arguably the best vocal coach in the world. Though he started his career helping singers, he has recently branched out and begun helping speakers. He says there is not much difference between singing and speaking. He helps his clients discover that they are not stuck with the voice they were born with, especially when that voice does not match their personality or business goals.

When I stepped into Roger's office, he spent the first quarter of an hour getting to know me and listening to my story. He affirmed my bubbly personality and informed me that my voice was not letting me fully shine in my interaction with others. My teeth were actually inhibiting any air from coming out, so I was failing to connect with anyone listening to me. He explained that our voices are gifts for others, not to be kept to ourselves. When we speak, air leaves our mouths and vibrates the listener. This vibration impacts one's emotions and plays a big role in the message being delivered. Roger's patient coaching began with getting rid of my old, unhelpful speaking habits before he could teach me to speak with more resonance.

In graduate school, there were times when professors invited my colleagues and me to unlearn something that had been hindering us from taking in new information. We had previously memorized a process and now we were presented with a more accurate one. We might have learned the long way when the shortcut was actually more consistent and appropriate in most situations. Whatever the case, it was understandably confusing to shift gears and learn a new way of doing things. As students, we adapted and grew accustomed to what worked in the past. Now, the professor challenged us to focus on a niche that would help in our specific fields.

INTIMACY IN THE DESERT

This shift reminds me of God's invitation into the desert. *Jesus does not chase us into the desert as a punishment but rather woos us into a quiet period of intimacy and reunion.* While we may try to grasp familiarity in the desert and make ourselves at home, God is in the process of leading us out by having us follow His timely steps. The desert is not our home.

Since I'm a Midwestern girl who has been to the desert only a couple of times in my life, I did some research on what sounds are like in that environment. I discovered a blogger who wrote, "The desert is a place of great stillness and a place that silence suits well.

And after all, sound is the most evanescent of all sensations—here and then gone in an instant, leaving no trace. To be deaf in the desert would be to become more a part of it—a place that displays time and timelessness in its every ancient feature. The events or sensations of an instant—or indeed of a lifetime—don't cut much mustard in such a place as this. But let me not mislead you: soundless does not equate to lifeless."[27]

Sound is not just audible; love is communicated at an even deeper level than what our sense of hearing experiences. Lovers can communicate without saying a word. During this season, I have gone on two silent retreats and have backpacked the Camino de Santiago in Spain. On the first retreat, I dove into _The Power of Silence_ by Cardinal Robert Sarah. It was astonishing to be reminded of how many beautiful and intimate moments in life are silent. I invite you to stop reading for a minute and make a mental list of some of these moments.

What did you come up with? Pretty crazy realization, right?

Cardinal Sarah writes, "Sounds and emotions detach us from ourselves, whereas silence always forces man to reflect upon his own life." When you are in a remote location on a clear, starry night, you may comment to a loved one nearby, "Wow! Look at the stars!" However, those words are not needed in order to experience the wonder and awe. Words can even interrupt the moment. There's an Alison Krauss lyric that tells the lover, "You say it best when you say nothing at all."

TURN DOWN THE VOLUME

In our homes and in our world, there is much unnecessary noise. The TV is turned on and the smartphones are dinging; the radio is blaring and children are fighting; spouses are seeking to be heard and understood rather than to listen and understand. We live in a society that runs from ourselves. Adolescents wear earbuds as if they are part of their ear; people keep the TV on for noise, so they don't feel alone at home; and it's hard to do any chore now without asking Alexa to play music or read an audiobook to listen to while you work.

In this season of single life, I have been better acquainted with myself because there is plenty of silence. I live alone with my two-

---

[27] http://www.consortiuminfo.org/standardsblog/articles/sounds-desert-silence

year-old cat. She doesn't make much noise beyond a purr or meow, but she's at least fun to talk to. She's good at listening. Unless I intentionally turn something on, my house is quiet. Growing up in a busy home with quads, I have always been good at entertaining myself. While my siblings shared a bedroom, I always savored my own room as a sanctuary. I have been independent since the beginning of my life, and I am grateful for that because it has helped me in single life. I can walk into social events by myself and have enjoyed spontaneously traveling alone.

I am an extroverted processor who often speaks to think. I have always been attracted to the compliment "She doesn't say much, but when she opens her mouth it's something of value." There is a rumor that introverts carry a mental word counter to monitor how much they speak in a day before they expire. As we are often intrigued by opposite personalities, I try to learn from this behavior in this season of waiting on God.

TUNING OUR EAR

God is always speaking, but He's not always speaking in ways we expect. This is similar to a partner communicating, but not always in the ways we are accustomed to. We get used to going through the motions and assuming we know what the other person is thinking, is feeling, or is about to say. Often, people can have a whole conversation in their heads before they even approach the person to initiate dialogue. This is not productive since the other person has yet to be invited to contribute.

Because God created us, He knows that we do this and invites us into a change of scenery to gain a new perspective. Have you noticed that you are inspired when you are on vacation or on a retreat? Or working on a project in your regular office space, as opposed to a trendy coffee shop across town? What if you move outside onto the porch rather than remain at your kitchen table? As humans we get accustomed to doing, hearing, and seeing things in a way that we have experienced before.

It is in this change that we grow more attuned to what is around us. It took a couple of years for me personally to adjust to the sounds outside my house. Now, I'm settled in and the urban noises don't faze me as much as they did. When I visit others' homes or offices, I seem to notice something that they hadn't noticed. Like these shifts in our environment, silence invites us to open ourselves to surprises and new discoveries. When people shake up a routine or filter out a noisy distraction, it can be both scary and thrilling because new things become possible. It can be scary because we may be asked to make a change of perspective. God provides the ultimate perspective through Our Lord, who knocks on the doors of our hearts. He hopes we answer and are able to hear His words of truth and love.

SURPRISES IN THE DESERT

God is constantly reminding us in little ways to not put Him in a box. He can communicate with us in ways that no human can. Though we are surrounded by noise and audible voices in the world, our hearts are made for the still, small voice of God. From the moment we were formed in our mother's womb, God was communicating with us. It is not until 18 weeks after conception that an unborn baby hears his or her first sound![28] So God must be speaking to our hearts before then in His own mysterious way. He is found in the unexpected as Elijah discovered Him—not in the wind, earthquake, or fire, but rather in the light silent sound:

> Then the LORD said: Go out and stand on the mountain before the LORD; the *LORD will pass by*. There was a strong and violent wind rending the mountains and crushing rocks before the LORD—but the LORD was not in the wind; after the wind, an earthquake—but the LORD was not in the earthquake; after the earthquake, fire—but the LORD was not in the fire; after the fire, *a light silent sound*. When he heard this, Elijah hid his face in his cloak and went out and stood at the entrance of the cave. A voice said to him, "Why are you here, Elijah?" He replied, "I have been most zealous for the LORD, the God of hosts, but the Israelites have forsaken your covenant. They have destroyed your altars and murdered your prophets by the sword. I alone remain, and they seek to take my life." The LORD said to him: Go back! *Take the desert road...*[29]

I like how the Lord invites Elijah to take the desert road. Walking is an opportunity to move away from what is familiar and be open to

[28] https://www.healthline.com/health/pregnancy/when-can-a-fetus-hear#1
[29] 1 Kings 19:11-15 (NABRE, emphasis added)

new sights and sounds. Along the desert road, my buddy Eli may have seen a cactus. While I was waiting to meet with my vocal coach, Roger Love, I ventured off of Hollywood Boulevard in downtown Los Angeles to get a glimpse of the famous Hollywood sign. A cactus blooming with flowers captured my attention! I have always had the expectation that cacti were just prickly, green, and dull. Yes, it's true. I've never been a huge fan of cacti even though my favorite color is green, and I've had fun memories at a bar with that name. Now, I am astonished by this beautiful plant that illustrates the surprises we find in the silence. It seems as though nothing is happening and then one day we recognize the yellow, orange, and pink blooms. What's incredible about this discovery is that I never would have seen the blooms if I hadn't gone for a walk off the beaten path. God is the coolest, isn't He?

God also appreciates a sense of humor. I have always enjoyed a meme that highlights a favorite quote from St. Joseph in Scripture. It reads, "____. " It takes a second to get it because it is not like other favorite quotes. St. Joseph is one of the most influential Saints, yet He is not quoted once in Scripture. He accepted his quiet role accompanying Mary and Jesus in family life. He was so practiced in listening that He even received messages from angels in his dreams! On their long journeys together as a family to Bethlehem and Egypt, they may not have talked as much as they listened. God is always speaking to us, and sometimes we just have to get out of the way so that we can hear Him. He doesn't necessarily speak the way we think either, and that can be frustrating. The silence can lead to feelings of loneliness or abandonment. However, those are feelings and not the whole truth. Jesus is the Good Shepherd and we are His sheep. He promises us, "He walks ahead of [us], and [we] follow him, because [we] recognize his voice."[30] He invites us to simply "be still and know that [He] is God."[31]

Reflection: How can you make space for more silence in your life?

---

[30] John 10:4 (NABRE)
[31] Psalm 46:11 (NABRE)

5

PATIENCE: WONDER IN THE WAITING

"O Lord, you have always been our home. Before you created the hills or brought the world into being, you were eternally God, and will be God forever. You tell us to return to what we were; you change us back to dust. A thousand years to you are like one day; they are like yesterday, already gone, like a short hour in the night."[32]

In addition to the Camino teaching me about silence, the pilgrimage also taught me about patience. It's neither a short nor an easy walk across Spain to reach the Cathedral of Santiago. In a world where speedy vehicles can get us from here to there quickly, it is countercultural to choose to walk. Almost every day is filled with unknown about where we would eat and reside for the evening. As cars and bicycles passed me by, I could only walk as fast as my feet would carry me. Going on a walk anywhere is a practice in patience, because you commit to a path and know that you will complete it no matter how long it takes.

During my walk on the Way, every sight and town I walked through was new for me, so I was able to wonder about what each would be like when I arrived. On that particular path, all pilgrims cultivate a wonder about Santiago, the destination. Some walk months and some only days, but all wonder about where the journey will take us. When I began this journey, I knew I would always be a pilgrim and would continue to see life in a more detached way as I grow to be more patient in the process.

---

[32] Psalm 90:1-4 (GNT)

GIFT OF SEASONS

One of my favorite things about being Catholic is living by the liturgical calendar. Every year I count on an Advent season inviting me to slow down as I wait for Christmas, and a Lenten season inviting me into the beautiful mystery of the desert to prepare my heart for Good Friday and Easter Sunday.

Silence   I am thrilled every Advent to reflect on waiting in joyful hope. It's a season that helps us push back against culture's pressure to plan, do, and fill our schedules. While department stores and businesses are deep in Christmas celebrations, the Church reminds us that we're not quite there yet. It is a powerful season for countering what "everyone" may be doing and remembering the intentionality of God's timing. There is beauty in the longing and in remembering what (and who) we are longing for. We are invited to offer up impatience to the reality that patience is not an easy virtue to grow.

Lent is another season of waiting as God calls us into the desert to grow in intimacy with Him. In Deuteronomy, God told the Israelites that He was always with them, even though they endured all types of challenges for 40 years! We think 40 days can last forever, especially as Midwestern weather imitates our internal battle in that winter doesn't go out without a fight. When the Bible mentions a number, it's more symbolic than literal. The number 40 is associated with testing—a faith that is not tested cannot be trusted.

God gives us these seasons every year to recollect ourselves and ask ourselves how we are aligning our lives with His will. When we hit adolescence, we are drawn to the opposite sex and wonder when it's our turn for someone to return our affection. I invite you to flip that observation and think about how God waits for you to turn back to Him. In a season of singleness, especially when there are one-sided feelings, we can put ourselves in God's shoes to get a glimpse of how He feels when we don't reciprocate His feelings.

LESSONS IN THE WAITING

A helpful quote to guide our mindset when we are waiting for something is to ask, "What am I learning while I'm waiting?" This culture does not like to wait. We tend to look for things to distract from or expedite the process. From Instapots to Instagram to Instacart, we want results to be instant. Most, if not all, people in a waiting room or checkout line are engrossed in their phone rather than feeling the tension of the wait.

When I'm waiting for an unknown, I can think of it as either scary or as exciting. It's scary because I realize I don't have control and I am assured that God's plan always includes suffering of some kind. He never said love is easy, but rather expressed His ever-patient love with us by stretching out His arms on the cross to carry the weight of *our* sins, not His. Since we don't have control, it can also be an exciting time, because anything is possible with God and He loves to surprise us with all that is good.

There is a beauty in waiting that does not make itself apparent until after the time has passed. I have never heard someone say after meeting someone with whom they shared physical chemistry that they were excited to wait for sex until marriage. No one is excited about the wait. Waiting is hard. It's really hard. Everything around us seems to justify "just do it" or "you deserve it now."

Financially, we are used to having a piece of plastic in our wallets that can "pay" for anything at any time, removing any need to save up cash for an item before purchasing. When was the last time you saved up for something and then could lay down the money on the counter knowing what you had to sacrifice or the work you endured to make it possible? What an achievement!

When I was growing up, we watched TV shows *live* and had to wait a whole week to watch the next episode! Shows were full of cliff-hangers, and it was a part of discussions with friends and family in anticipation for the rest of the story to continue. Now, people binge-watch TV shows and can dive into a whole season in one day. No reason for cliff-hangers or conversations about each episode.

In the Catholic Church, we prepare adults seeking Baptism or 1st Communion through a yearlong process called Rite of Christian Initiation for Adults (RCIA). They experience Jesus week by week as catechumens and candidates increase their knowledge of Church history and tradition. *When we learn about Jesus, we learn about ourselves.*

Culture teaches us that to want is to receive. The Church reminds us that good things take time, and it is a powerful experience to journey with those in RCIA. It is indeed a long process, but I have yet to hear a neophyte (a new convert) say they wish it was not that long. They are always grateful for the preparation and are full of joy to receive the Sacraments at Easter Vigil. It wasn't just handed to them. They had to engage in some commitments and sacrifices while also wrestling with questions still needing to be answered in their hearts.

BUILDING TRUST

Since the Church represents the Bride of Christ, this waiting period can cross over into the dating and engagement process as well when you meet someone you want to get to know better. Most of the time, two people don't marry immediately after meeting. Typically, a couple dates for years and then enters into a season of engagement when they prepare for their lives together. Then, finally, after some time of getting to know one another come to the altar to join their lives together. In this time of journeying together, they grow in knowledge of and love for their partner and his or her family and friends. There's an element of trust that is built.

God trusts us as we wonder in the waiting.

Yes, God not only loves you, but also likes you and trusts you. He asks you to be patient to make sure that the best gifts have time to be given in perfection.

Writing this chapter while sitting at a coffee shop reminds me of how delicious concoctions take time to create. A little of this and a little of that is warmed, distilled, steamed, or iced. The barista wants the customer to have the drink they asked for and wants to make sure it is served with perfection. How much more does our Father in Heaven want to serve His children with perfection!

As a marriage counselor, I have been eager to have a partner of my own, so I can help reveal God's loving plan of marriage to the world. Yet God's plan for me now in my season of singleness is to live in His love knowing that He is currently working everything together for my good. He spoils His children and grants them the desires of His heart. He loves us so much that He won't give any gift at any time other than the perfect time.

I've studied the interaction between God and our first parents in the garden. God ordered them to not *take* from the tree, not because He was holding out on them, but because He wanted to *give* them the food in due time. Only God can satisfy our desires because He knows our hearts better than we do and created us for relationship with Him. God wants to grow in relationship with you. Isn't that a wild concept to try to comprehend?

On a flight home from a family vacation, I thought about the different energy expended on the trip to the destination as compared to the trip home. When planning a trip, all travelers correspond over details about transportation, hotel, and things to do. Some personalities find joy in doing research about the destination, others discover the best deals, and still others simply revel in the excitement. Everyone blocks off their calendar ahead of time to create space to get away. Relationships grow closer through more frequent contact prior to the trip as they share needs, preferences, and feelings.

I remember receiving a message on Facebook from a girl in Wisconsin suggesting that we become roommates in our first year at Saint Mary's College. We were not moving to campus for months yet, but our mutual "yes" initiated a friendship that is still deepening more than a decade later. Her vulnerable invitation comforted me as I prepared to transition from high school to college. I knew I had someone in my court who wanted to know me and share life with me.

When a couple wants to get married, they enter a season of engagement…where they *engage* with one another on a deeper level. There is a sense of "already but not yet." In the Church, this season includes various types of preparation. While planning the wedding, the couple discovers the differences in their personalities and how they work together. They take an inventory about their family of origin, values, and expectations for marriage. These results help to guide discussions in meetings with pastors and sponsor couples who mentor the couple through the transition. Though each partner obviously thinks they know one another enough to commit to one another for a lifetime, there is always something new to unveil about a person. We cannot be fully understood and thus always remain a mystery, even to a spouse of 70 years! As we curiously ask a loved one a question about them, it helps us to reflect on our own answer. In learning about others, we learn more about ourselves. If there's someone with whom you find it difficult to coexist, it is likely that there is a part of them that reminds you of a part of you that you don't like.

Though we are eager to jump to the next step or topic on our mind, we learn so much when we can wait to journey with others rather than jumping ahead of others.

FULLNESS OF JOY

One of my weaknesses in my past relationship was waiting for marriage. I had an understanding that I was not fulfilled as a single woman. I idolized marriage and envisioned a completion of life and joy after the vows were made! Boy, was I wrong.

> *God does not withhold His joy from us in any season. He is fully present with us now, regardless of our relationship status.*

Recently in a homily, the priest focused on the completion of joy in our lives today. Jesus said, "I have told you this so that my joy may be in you and your joy may be complete"[33] One of the episodes of *The Office* is titled "Did I Stutter?" This phrase is used when a clear message is not received by an audience. When Jesus says, "Your joy may be complete," he does not stutter or use any conditions. He doesn't say, "...when you are in a romantic relationship," or "...when you are married." Jesus provides the fullness of His grace for us today as we open ourselves up and ask for it. Often in times of waiting, we pray for anyone but ourselves. We plan for a season that we are not in. We live for a day we haven't yet seen. Life is about the journey. Not the destination.

I have recognized that the coaches I gravitate toward are incredibly present in the moment and thus connect well with their clients and audiences. While onstage with one of them recently, I learned about the Alexander Technique.[34] Our bodies are made to be flexible and present to challenges we face. The more stressed and tense we become, the less we feel comfortable in our own skin. During the exercises, we got acquainted with our joints and how we can move more freely. One of the most powerful experiences was simple. We repeated the phrase, "I have time." Our bodies immediately responded to that stated reality and relaxed.

As someone who wrestles with anxiety in my daily life, I often worry about unnecessary things and am rushed for no reason. On daily walks to a conference in San Diego's La Jolla Village, friends

---

[33] John 15:11 (NABRE)
[34] https://www.alexandertechnique.com/

and I stopped along the quaint sidewalks to admire and smell the flowers in people's front yards. The flowers had vibrant colors and calming scents—details we would have missed if we had walked on by. The ability to determine what matters and what doesn't is essential for finding peace each and every day. If the world is truly in God's hands and if His grace is in every moment, we truly do have time to enjoy the fullest of joy right now. Jesus invited those He encountered to slow down and get out of their heads and allow themselves to be present.

HOLY DARKNESS

On Good Friday this year, my parish sang "Holy Darkness." The lyrics express a dialogue between us and God:

> You and me: "Holy darkness, blessed night, heaven's answer hidden from our sight. As we await you, O God of silence, we embrace your holy night."

> God: "I have taught your soul to grieve. In the barren soil of your loneliness, there I will plant my seed."

Though we know that the Resurrection is coming, I am reminded of the first Easter when the world waited all weekend before discovering that the tomb was empty. Those people didn't have the concerns we do today as we plan Easter meals and attire. They likely reminded themselves of all that Jesus had told them. Had they missed something? How could Jesus be dead? This couldn't be the end of the story, could it?

There are many seasons in our lives when we are asked to wait. In order to plant a garden in our hearts, God has to first plant a seed and then watch it grow. This process is not a fast one, but it's a fulfilling one. The flowers that fill a church on Easter show us that the wait was worth it. We just had to have faith and hope in the darkness when we waited to see the light.

Reflection: What are you currently waiting on? How can you practice patience this week?

6

FAITH: BELIEVE IN WHAT IS NOT SEEN

"You created every part of me; you put me together in my mother's womb. I praise you because you are to be feared; all you do is strange and wonderful. I know it with all my heart. When my bones were being formed, carefully put together in my mother's womb, when I was growing there in secret, you knew that I was there—you saw me before I was born. The days allotted to me had all been recorded in your book, before any of them ever began."[35]

At the turn of the millennium, I became an avid fan of Derek Jeter from the New York Yankees. My copy of his autobiography developed wear and tear in my backpack as I read it multiple times. In it, he shares the story about how at the young age of eight years old he told his parents that he would one day play shortstop for the Yankees. Rather than telling him the low probability of boys his age accomplishing this audacious feat, his parents helped him to develop structure in his days to pave the way for his dream to be made a reality. As an ambitious junior high kid, reading his life story, I wished I had as clear a goal as he had. In high school, I discovered my desire to integrate psychology and faith. I embraced this and set out on the journey to reach it.

I attended Saint Mary's College to study psychology and religious studies; I then went on to Notre Dame to earn an MA in theology and then to Indiana Wesleyan to earn an MA in marriage counseling. At my five-year college reunion, I shared this story with

---

[35] Psalm 139: 13-16 (GNT)

an auditorium packed with alumnae as we welcomed a new president to our college community. When I was entering adolescence, I had no idea what was ahead for me. At that point, I was still sure that I was going to follow my family tradition and attend Indiana University. I didn't even know Saint Mary's College existed when I made my goal. Today, I am working as a marriage and family counselor and am writing this book integrating my life and my faith. I did not see the road ahead, but after learning how someone (Derek Jeter) realized his dream, I knew good things could be in store for me too.

BLIND FAITH

Faith. St. Paul defines faith as "the realization of what is hoped for and evidence of things not seen."[36] He explains that "we live by faith, not by sight."[37] On this side of heaven, we do not see the face of God in His fullness. We are asked to have faith that the best is yet to come and that what He promises will be fulfilled. Boy, isn't that a challenge during the season of single life? Relationship status can get us tied up in what God is really promising us. God promises everyone will find a spouse, right? Yes, but not in the way we often think.

Christ promises that He will satisfy our deepest desires and will draw us to Himself, our eternal Bridegroom. The problem with our interpretation is that *we get so tied up with our desires that we make our gifts the guide rather than the Giver.* I'll be the first to admit that I am scared to have faith in what I cannot see because I cannot see it! I like to know what's coming up on the horizon, and it's challenging to see something with my heart that I cannot see with my eyes. St. James warns against doubt, "When you ask, you must believe and not doubt, because the one who doubts is like a wave of the sea, blown and tossed by the wind."[38] We must have faith!

One of my favorite stories in Scripture is found in the second chapter of John's Gospel. Mary had watched her son grow up in front of her eyes. She knew that He was the Lord even though He hadn't revealed that Himself. She hadn't seen any miracles beyond conceiving her Beloved Son without the help of her husband. On

---

[36] Hebrews 11:1 (NABRE)
[37] 2 Cor 5:7 (NIV)
[38] James 1:6 (NIV)

the third day of a wedding feast of which Mary and Jesus were guests, she recognized that the wine was running low. If the wine ran out during the feast, it would bring shame and embarrassment on the newlywed couple. It's hard enough to predict the amount of food and drinks for a party or wedding reception that lasts just an evening. This wedding likely lasted about seven days.[39] Mary saw a need and had faith that Jesus could provide a solution, so she courageously asked Him for help. As the first disciple, Mary was challenged to believe even when she didn't see or understand. Her trust in Jesus never wavered.

It is curious to notice that this need was realized before the newlyweds were even aware of it three days into their reception. Thus, they did not have the opportunity to worry about the possibility of the disaster. This all happened behind the scenes while they enjoyed the festivities. The guests expected the usual parts of the celebration of drinking, feasting, and dancing, but sure would not have expected to witness a miracle. It wasn't just any miracle, either; it was Jesus' first miracle that would kick-start His public ministry across the whole land. He freely chose the small town of Cana at a wedding where the couple is not even recognized by name. If you ever feel insignificant or forgotten, this story can bring light in any darkness you may be experiencing. Our faith gives us the confidence that good things are coming even when we can't see or don't feel seen.

TRANSFORMATION

In order for good things to come, we need time to be transformed into a worthy vessel for the best. Jesus answered His mother's request to help the couple by ordering the servers to fill up jugs to the brim with water. When they sampled the water, it had become wine! It was of even better quality than the wine they had been drinking throughout the reception. This story would not have the same impact if it had happened at any other time, because this was the chosen time. In Matthew's Gospel, we learn that people don't "put new wine into old wineskins; otherwise, the wineskins burst, and the wine pours out and the wineskins are ruined, but they put

---

[39] https://www.bible-history.com/biblestudy/marriage.html

new wine into fresh wineskins, and both are preserved."[40]
Jesus wants to make all things new through the Father and the Holy Spirit. With time, God creates in us a new wineskin in which He can fill us to the brim with new wine. His goal for us is to become holy like Him so that we can be reunited with the Father in Heaven.

A Lenten series about God's will emphasized the importance of knowing three characteristics of God. He is omniscient (all-knowing), omnipotent (all-powerful), and good (benevolent). Usually, when we are growing anxious in the unknown, we are beginning to doubt one or more of these truths about our Father.

In counseling sessions, I often hear clients mention that they would not have been so compatible with their spouse if they had met at another time in their lives. Others reflect how transformative counseling was for them and how they might have never come in the first place if their heart was never breaking. These clients begin to see how timing is truly part of the big picture. We are all invited to have an eternal perspective as we become more aware of how God is working all things together for our good.[41]

It has felt weird to me at times to hear myself talk about my gratitude for my breakup. The pain and confusion have introduced me to new depths of emotion, hope, and empathy. Reaching the lowest point of hopelessness preceded my constant leaning on God to carry me to my current life where my heart is full of faith, hope, and love as I ponder His perfect will in my journey each day. Some days the wineskin analogy might not fit, but the imagery of the potter is always encouraging. Clay can get smashed, molded, and cracked, but the potter is a master and is delightfully creating a masterpiece.

For an artist, presence in the moment is critical. If painters are not honest about what is in front of them, they are not able to appreciate and add to what is on the canvas. Rather, they would possibly include some dried paint or miss the canvas altogether. A quote that often helps direct those looking for a purpose in life is finding "the point at which your gifts meet the world's need." If we don't know what the priority is, we don't know where to invest attention and energy.

---

[40] Matthew 9:17 (NASB)
[41] Romans 8:28 (NASB)

MIXED SIGNALS

From the single's perspective, I admit being lost in narratives that weren't reality. While I liked a guy and planned on his reciprocated affection in the months ahead, I didn't even stop to realize that we were not just on different pages, but in different stories altogether. Faith is indeed believing in what is not seen, but that doesn't mean making a person or relationship something that it isn't. The only truth we know is in the present because that is where God meets us. When we are lost in an imaginary future, we miss the invitations in the present.

As humans created by love and for love, we latch on to possible love stories in which we could feel beloved. Yet as St. Augustine says, "Our hearts are restless, Lord, until they rest in you." Unless we rest in the Christian story, where Christ pursues and saves His Bride through sacrificial love, we will feel heartbroken, confused, and disoriented trying to find satisfaction in one-sided love affairs. In addition to my own testimony of this struggle, I have heard of countless stories where people hope against hope in relationships. Indeed, "nothing is impossible with God."[42] But confusion does not come from God. If a man is interested in a woman romantically, he will be naturally moved to pursue her in some way. If he is not interested, he will not. Being on the receiving end, it is neither easy to wait for this pursuit nor easy to accept disinterest.

In *Love and Respect*, Dr. Emerson Eggerichs writes about the importance of respect for men and love for women. Though this can be controversial on feminine and masculine communication styles, it's been amazing to intentionally communicate respect for a male partner and watch him light up. One of the ways women can show respect is through letting the man guide the relationship. In their nature, men need to feel they are trusted and encouraged in the role of pursuer. Men don't want to be pushed or forced in a direction they are not ready to take on. Women feel loved when they are communicated with honestly and gently. In this communication, women are shown that they are worthy of pursuit and respected along the way.

To help both parties know the reality of what is in front of them, honest communication is essential. There are too many friendships

---

[42] Luke 1:37 (NASB)

out there that concern one party being much more invested than the other. This is usually due to obscure or vague boundaries that can easily be interpreted in multiple ways by the two individuals involved and by members of the community in which the "couple" belong.

TRUSTING JESUS

Jesus is a gentleman and is always open to communication. We are invited to come to Him to discuss our thoughts and feelings and listen to what He wants to say. He will neither lead us on nor manipulate our emotions. We need to have faith that He is the perfect guide!

In the movie *Christopher Robin*, Winnie the Pooh's wisdom astonished me and invited me to a deeper faith in the unknown. He says, "I get to where I am going by walking away from where I have been." Sometimes, Jesus simply asks us to take the next step forward. The path will be unveiled along the way. Pooh describes his favorite day as "today because tomorrow is too much day for me." This reminds me of a popular Scripture passage, "Do not worry about tomorrow; tomorrow will take care of itself."[43] With faith in God, we can rest in His loving presence today with complete trust that He will provide in the days ahead.

Reflection: How would you describe your trust in Jesus right now? What do you need from Him?

---

[43] Matthew 6:34 (NABRE)

III

Love Is Fruitful:
Your Life Matters

7

CHOOSE THE STRUGGLE; DON'T STRUGGLE WITH THE CHOICE

"Lord, I have given up my pride and turned away from my arrogance. I am not concerned with great matters or with subjects too difficult for me. Instead, I am content and at peace. As a child lies quietly in its mother's arms, so my heart is quiet within me. Israel, trust in the Lord now and forever!"[44]

I graduated from high school with three varsity letters in a sport I had not played before my sophomore year. My favorite sport was and still is volleyball. The joy I feel on the court is unlike what I feel on any other court, field, or green. I feel confident in my height, encouraged in my strength, and grateful to have to run only small spurts at a time. As a graduate of a small Catholic grade school entering a huge, public high school, I prayed to make the freshman volleyball team so that I could get to know other students before the first day of school. That prayer was answered with a fun season on the freshman volleyball team. The next years would not prove so smooth. After trying out for JV, I received a rejection letter from the coach. My plans of playing volleyball throughout high school came to a heartbreaking end.

I am not one to settle for doing nothing, so I sought an alternative option. I heard that there were only a couple of girls on the golf team and decided it would be a fun choice to be outside on beautiful fall days instead of staying home and grieving the year

---

[44] Psalm 131:1-3 (GNT)

without volleyball.

I borrowed my dad's clubs and headed to the driving range to hit my first bucket of golf balls with a club other than a putter. My previous golf experience included hitting a ball through lighthouse fixtures and tunnels on Putt-Putt courses. I don't remember struggling too much with this choice because I wanted to make the most out of high school regardless of whether the head volleyball coach would accept me on his team. Thankfully, there was a Catholic Youth Organization (CYO) volleyball league for high school students that year, too! I will admit that I continued to try out for volleyball at my high school in my junior year as well. With each and every apology letter from the head coach, I chose to go back out on the green to meet my fellow golfers. I learned the difference between clubs and improved my swing. Though I never won a match in my career, I received three varsity letters that will forever remind me of my choice to live life to the fullest.

TOO MANY FISH IN THE SEA

Choosing love is a real struggle because it is not easy. It is different than choosing what sport to play in high school, and the viable options we have in this world can be paralyzing. People often make a choice with poor judgment or don't make a choice at all when it comes to love. In this society, love is understood as transient. Recreational sex and no-fault divorce highlight this reality as partners seem to change as often as someone's favorite song or software update. A phrase I often hear in breakup advice is, "There are more fish in the sea." There are so many fish that we are not able to focus on one for long. Have you ever watched a school of fish swim through an aquarium? If you've had the opportunity to snorkel or dive in the ocean, you have seen many fish! It's almost impossible to keep your eye on just one because reflections from others' movements or scales are distracting. There are so many!

I'm now thinking of all the varieties of pizza. When a favorite pizza place closes, someone can try to comfort you by saying that there is more pizza around town. Well, that is an obvious statement. Of course, there is pizza, but you enjoyed ordering this one unique combination at this place on the corner with the great patio that allowed you to enjoy your pizza pie in the sunshine with your dog nearby. There are veggie pizzas, meat pizzas, dessert pizzas, and breakfast pizzas, just to name a few. After living in Italy, I have even noticed a difference between ordering in Rome and ordering at home in Indiana. There is even a difference between pizza in New York and pizza in Chicago. So, clearly, there is a difference between topping combinations and the place from which you order. Being told that there are other options doesn't provide comfort as you grieve your lost option.

WHAT TO CHOOSE

Aziz Ansari wrote in his book, *Modern Romance*, that it was easier for his dad to find his wife 30 years ago in an arranged marriage after a couple of meetings than it is for Aziz to decide what he wants for dinner. This is comical because it's true to the point that it's uncomfortable to think about. He writes about the difficulty of modern dating now, because someone can have thousands of contacts in their pocket while they are sitting face-to-face with a date. Is this the best person? Is this date worth it? What if someone better messages me this week? These are questions that are not far off or even irrelevant. This is the reality that this culture faces.

According to Barry Schwartz, there is a "Paradox of Choice." It is helpful to have options so that we can be free to choose. However, we now have too many options and are often exhausted with making any choice at all. In Barry's book, he gives practical steps to decrease the number of decisions we make each day so that we can be less stressed, anxious, and busy.

LOVING THE LOST SHEEP

When loved ones try to console me with, "There are many fish in the sea," I feel an emptiness inside. The emptiness is not about the falsity of the statement, but rather the sadness of this understanding of love. The story of the 99 sheep is so radical for us because we point out that there are 99 others! Yes, there are 99 others, but 1 is missing. My experience of romantic love has taught me a lot about Christ's pursuit of us, His Bride. We sometimes do not feel worthy and run off to hide. Society would say, "Oh well, there are others, so we can forget about that one."

Though I agree that there can be unhealthy attachments and denial in the grieving process, I pose counterarguments for this way of thinking from professional and personal experience. As a marriage counselor, I hear about many marriages being broken when a partner leaves for their first love. As a Christian, I learn that receiving love is about giving love. As a woman in love, I feel that this phrase is disrespectful of the relationship and the beloved.

Using the analogy of the sheep, there are many reasons a sheep might be lost, just like there are many conclusions as to how a relationship ended. The Gospel doesn't say whether the sheep ran away on purpose or accidentally, or what its personality was like. Maybe it was a pain and annoying, but maybe it was the cutest lamb in the bunch—just got lost a lot.

PONDER IN YOUR HEART

Our Mother Mary teaches us to "ponder in our hearts" and listen to our thoughts, feelings, and interactions. In the Old Testament, there were many times when the people panicked when plans seemed to change, and sometimes when people waited on the next move.

What God has never told us is to "stop loving." We may set more boundaries or develop healthy patterns to remain open to God's will in our lives when our relationships change. More than anything in this breakup experience, I have experienced the true power of love. Praying for my ex, his heart, and his sanctity has been a great joy amid the darkness. I feel as though I'm called to be a prayer warrior from afar to love him through prayers. And until God changes my heart, I will continue to love him even when I don't always understand why or what the fruit of this love will be.

Some say, "What if loving him makes you miss out on someone who can love you back?" Well, of course I want to be loved. However, love is not all about what we get. And I would rather love him fully than love someone simply to have someone to love. As my heart is aching for the love I lost, it is even more clear for me when I sit in front of a couple who are complaining about one another rather than expressing their love and gratitude. When this happens, I usually invite them to recall their first date and when they first fell in love with one another.

This reminder noticeably changes the vibe in the room. They begin to smile and laugh a bit as fond memories surprisingly return. Love is like the spring of eternal life. As love grows, it transforms aridity into abundance. If I forget to drink water for hours at a time,

I lose energy and become light-headed. Though I am made of water, to consume water, and to give water to others, I can't survive the day without drinking it myself. I can't magically be hydrated. I have to fill up a glass and work to consume it. Love takes work too.

CHOOSING LOVE

My clients have exhibited some unhealthy understandings of choosing love. It may be interpreted somewhat similar to choosing an iPhone. Yes, you chose that particular phone, but what about when a new phone comes out—you will likely want to switch, right? Arranged marriages can illustrate how a choice alone can be honored, cherished, and life-giving. Love is about commitment. Pope Francis has encouraged young people to make choices in life. This sounds inevitable, but the reality is that people do not make important choices in life because of analysis paralysis.

The most successful people choose to do something, rather than nothing. Many successful entrepreneurs advise that they have gotten to where they are today by taking the next best step again and again until they reach their goals. Some have described this by starting with a goal and working backward to see what action can be made now to move the needle in the future. After you've chosen an action step, there is room for growth and learning in the process. In *The One Thing*, Gary Keller argues that it's not about being busier, but rather being less distracted from your main goal. When it comes to making decisions in life, we welcome distractions (sometimes unconsciously) so that we can procrastinate on focusing and eliminating options.

THE BEST YES

One of the books I recommend most is *The Best Yes*. Lysa TerKeurst presents the reality that there are many good options, but often one that is best. We wear many hats in our work and family lives. We encounter invitations daily to answer God's nudges as His vessel of grace for others. We cannot be all things to all people all the time. Knowing that means that some no's will be necessary. In fact, *every yes begins with a no*! By getting out of bed, we are saying no to sleeping longer. By saying yes to a girls' night out, we are saying no to a quiet night in. Every purchase means you are saying no to saving. When an audience attends an event, they are saying no to doing anything else. We can be present in only one place at one time, and it's humbling to realize how often our no provides space for our yes. When we say yes to spend a lifetime with a partner, we are saying no to others who may come into our lives. At some point, though, if we want to be married, we need to say yes to someone.

In one of the final episodes of *The Office*, undoubtedly one of my favorite TV shows, Dwight and Jim have a short interchange on love as Dwight prepares to propose to Angela. Because Jim and his wife, Pam, are clear role models of a fun and fulfilling marriage, Jim says the following to Dwight:

> Jim: "I don't know what you want me to tell you, man. All I know is that every time I've been faced with a tough decision, there's only one thing that outweighs every other concern. One thing that will make you give up on everything you thought you knew. Every instinct, every rational calculation."
>
> Dwight: "Some sort of virus?"
>
> Jim: "Love."
>
> Dwight: "Oh."
>
> Jim: "Dwight, listen: No matter what happens, you gotta forget about all the other stuff, you gotta forget about logic and fear and doubt. You just gotta do everything you can to get to the one woman who's gonna make all this work. At the end of the day, you gotta jump."

Love is not easy, but it's so worth it to wake up with someone who chose you for life. You chose to spend your life together! Your partner for LIFE! Do we get a handbook on this radical love? Yes, in fact. The Bible is a love letter that helps us learn about how God chose us and invites us to choose Him. He is a very jealous God who asks us to be completely faithful in our choice without putting any other gods before Him.

No matter who is by our side, God wants to be our number one. When we recognize that we are choosing something or someone to point us to God rather than replace God, our decisions are a little less daunting. As we make choices each day, we can ask for God's guidance and faith in following through.

Tori Kelly offers a beautiful prayer in her song "Soul's Anthem":

65

Teach me how to love You / Show me how to trust You / More than with my words or with a song / No, it's not been easy / To live life down on my knees / But with faith I know I'll carry on / There is more to see than with my eyes / But fear sometimes can leave me paralyzed / I realize that I'm not in control / Yet it is well with my soul

Reflection: What has helped you choose love? What has made it difficult to choose love in your life?

8

A SPOUSE IS AN ASSIST, NOT THE GOAL

"God, be merciful to us and bless us; look on us with kindness, so that the whole world may know your will; so that all nations may know your salvation. May all the peoples praise you, O God; may all the peoples praise you![45]

When I was in a romantic relationship, my friends often challenged me to dream beyond marriage. After I'd idolized marriage, my vision for my future was focused on tying the knot and I couldn't see much else past that point. Though I have a God-given longing to be a wife and mother, loved ones were reminding me that those roles will never be the sum of my identity. Since my breakup, I have learned so much about my personal story and gifts, and how both can impact the world regardless of whether I have a ring on my finger or a baby in my womb.

Our main goal is to get to heaven and to inspire others to follow the God who created our deepest desires, the God who is Love Himself. On this journey, we live out vocations. Vocation comes from the word *vocare*, which means "to call." Marriage is one of the seven Sacraments of the Church and it falls under the category of Service. Thus, the mission of marriage is to serve your spouse and your family as you journey together toward heaven. Marriage is not the goal and it's not for everyone. That's one of the many reasons why there are higher divorce rates in the Church. It's a calling from God, who knows your deepest needs and desires. When we see

---

[45] Psalm 67:1-3 (GNT)

marriage as the goal, we grasp at it and begin to act as though we deserve it.

ABUNDANT MINDSET

At my stage in life, it feels as if I hear of an engagement, a wedding, or a pregnancy almost daily. To be completely honest, I thought of these as a threat to my own journey. If someone else is getting married, then that lowers my chance, right? God is a God of abundance and not of scarcity. Our paths with our peers are parallel. Someone else's success does not mean I failed and vice versa. If we are all obsessed with being the one to plan the next wedding that will look great on Pinterest boards, we will miss the calling and the gift amid the champagne and expensive dresses.

As a baseball fan, I appreciated the analogy of a batting average in dating. A batting average is calculated by "dividing a player's hits by his total at-bats for a number between zero (shown as .000) and one (1.000). In recent years, the Major League Baseball batting average has typically hovered around .260."[46] So the most revered professional baseball players get a hit about 3 times in every 10 at-bats. When preparing for marriage, a person needs only one partner. So, in that light, those who are "single and ready to mingle" need only 1 hit out of 10 or more dating experiences. With an acceptable batting average that low in the dating scene, we do not have to focus on marriage being a goal. Rather, it's a surprise in the game of life when the ball connects with the bat, and even more so when the ball leaves the park for a home run.

Author, blogger, and speaker Stephanie May Wilson, who has played a big role in my new perspective on singleness, encourages singles to find passion and purpose in their season and follow their heart where it takes them. Do you want to travel or do more service work? Do you want to accept that new job across the country? Do you want to get a new pet? These decisions are just examples of things that help us to be authentic to live the life we feel called to without holding back in fear of missing an opportunity to meet a spouse back home. People often say, "It's a small world." It truly is a small world when we let God guide our steps in and out of one another's lives. If we are called to marriage, doing mission work or

---

[46] http://m.mlb.com/glossary/standard-stats/batting-average

moving for a job will not inhibit meeting a spouse. It will not only increase your social network of people with others who share the same interests but also provide the space to connect with a future partner while you're doing what you love.

POTENTIAL AHEAD

Sometimes while driving I can get distracted with something in my rearview mirror. I quickly remind myself that what is in front of me is more important than what is behind me. Those whom God calls to journey with us will meet us where we are, so we are free to continue on our way to living life to the fullest. If we hold up or backtrack on our goals in order to manage the timeline of our love story, we will not be stepping into our potential of who God is calling us to be.

One of the most influential examples of stepping into personal potential is St. Peter. In Scripture, we learn that he cared for his mother-in-law. This relationship hints at his marriage. We are not certain about his wife's story, but we know that Peter did not identify himself by his marriage. Rather, he dropped everything and followed Christ. The Greek meaning of the name Peter is "rock."[47] Jesus built His Church on the rock of faith that Peter had in his friend whom He followed. It is curious to learn that "to peter" means to diminish gradually and come to an end.[48] Though imperfect like the rest of us, Peter modeled his life after Christ and lived for God's glory.

ETERNAL PERSPECTIVE

While I was finishing this book, a colleague of mine was killed in an accident on the way home from a grad school reunion we attended together. She was five years younger than me and grieving her passing has helped me to refocus on the purpose of our earthly life. We never know when God will call us home. If we become fixated on a certain condition or situation in our lives, we might miss the bigger picture God is illustrating through our lives. Ultimately, my goal is to get to Heaven and in the meantime live each day for God's glory. My colleague died single, reminding me that a spouse is not

---

[47] http://www.thinkbabynames.com/meaning/1/Peter
[48] https://www.merriam-webster.com/dictionary/peter

going to fulfill me. If God has other plans in store for me, I want to offer my yes to Him.

There is a famous legend that took place before Peter was crucified in Rome. He left the city and encountered Christ carrying the cross walking in the opposite direction. He asked Jesus, "Quo vadis?"—translated, "Where are you going?" Jesus told him he was going to Rome to be crucified again. In this moment, Peter turned around and offered His life in love for Christ. This reminds me of John 6, when Jesus' teachings seemed so burdensome for His disciples that they departed from Christ. He turned to Peter and asked if he was going to go as well. Peter replied, "To whom shall we go? You have the words of eternal life."

Only God gives us eternal life. Loved ones can point us to Christ through their love, prayers, and reminders of Truth. When we begin to place anything or anyone ahead of Christ, let us ask, "Quo vadis?" and turn our hearts back to Him.

Reflection: How are your relationships limiting what you believe is possible with God?

9

TRANSITIONAL SINGLE LIFE

"But as for me, I will pray to you, Lord; answer me, God, at a time you choose. Answer me because of your great love, because you keep your promise to save... Answer me, Lord, in the goodness of your constant love; in your great compassion turn to me!"[49]

Sitting in a pew in the National Shrine of the Immaculate Conception watching my friend get ordained to the priesthood, I noticed there were a lot of children, like *a lot*. I was still processing the conversation I'd had with my friend on the drive to the church. I'd told her about my book and what I have learned during my yearlong dating fast. I have been really wrestling with God about how He can use me in this season. I have a big baby itch and am eager to become a mother and wife. In the middle of the liturgy, a family in front of me turned around and asked if I wanted to hold their infant daughter. I replied, "*Yes!* Yes, I do!" Little Hellen was so content in my arms and I embraced her little frame as the bread and wine were consecrated into the Body and Blood of Christ. Brother Joseph was no longer a deacon and was standing beside Bishop Barron at the altar for the first time as Father Joseph. My friend beside me was approaching her second wedding anniversary. And there I was, a single woman in my 30s surrounded by families full of life and love.

As I'm waiting for God to bring me to my own wedding day, I

---

49 Psalm 69:13, 16 (GNT)

can help others in their vocations. I can pray for my friend who is now a priest. I can help a couple focus during a homily by holding their baby at Mass. It's a win-win situation, right?! There is definitely a purpose for this season, and I don't want to wake up months from now realizing I missed the opportunities to love now.

CALLED TO JOY

As a catechetical leader in the Church, I helped adults bring life to faith and faith to life. If you grew up in Catholic education, you probably heard about vocations often. The highlighted vocations are married life, priesthood, and religious life. At times you might hear of consecrated single life in the mix. These ways of life present a road map for holiness. It can be scary to imagine God just handing you the map whether you want it or not. Well, first of all, this is scary because it's not how God works. God is rich in mercy and has created us to live a life to the full. If we will not experience true joy in one of these paths, God will not ask us to take a lifelong vow to pursue it. That's pretty cruel. As Fr. Jim Gallagher often announced after dorm Masses at the University of Notre Dame, God wants to invite us on the path that offers us deep and lasting joy.

Today there is a poor understanding of this invitation to joy, as evidenced by the marriages that are depressing and dissolving. Contrary to popular belief, not everyone is called to the Sacrament of Marriage. Those who aren't called to say "I do" on a wedding day can receive and give love in other unique ways. Priests give their life for the Bride of Christ, the Church, as they bring the Eucharist to the People of God. The men and women who join religious orders as a Brother or a Sister commit to a dedicated life of prayer for the world as we all prepare for the heavenly marriage to come. Then, we have single life. The Church really struggles with this area because it's more vague than the avenues just mentioned. Many people ask how singleness can be a vocation, yet there are many Saints who lived a life of singleness. In this chapter, my focus is on discovering holiness in a transitional season of singleness rather than a lifelong consecration to sacred single life.

IN TRANSITION

Priests in formation enter a yearlong period of transitional diaconate.

They don't remain there permanently like those married men who become Permanent Deacons. The priests-in-formation are called a deacon only for a time, before they take their final vows. I want to explore what a transitional single life looks like as one seeks holiness before taking a vow.

Transitional single life: a season in which a man or woman is single yet does not feel called to be single forever. They do not fit into any vocational category but are living a life of holiness right where they are.

Transitional single life is not a vocation like transitional deaconate because no vows are made. They are alike, however, as paths to holiness that remind us that we discover God where we are and anticipate Him with joyful hope in where He is leading us. A single person in this season is not yet married, ordained, or consecrated, but looks for a place in the community as they wait actively on God's plan to be revealed.

Catholic young adult ministry is one of the most necessary and complicated undertakings in our modern Church, because this is where most of the people in this category fall. Young adulthood is a season of unknown that includes college graduation, moving to new places, starting or switching jobs, forming identity and relationships, and developing an independent perspective on religiosity and spirituality. After a young adult has spent four years around a population that is almost exclusively peers, the "real world" can be intimidating and disheartening. Questions like "Wait, I don't get to spend all day in a coffee shop studying with my friends anymore?" or "How do you make friends when you have to travel farther than a hallway of open doors?" or "Who am I now that my wardrobe does not solely include spirit wear from my alma mater?"

ECHOING LOVE IN EACH SEASON

When I was graduating from Saint Mary's College, I was ecstatic to be offered a coveted and competitive spot in a graduate program at Notre Dame across the street. This program was a hybrid of sorts that provided a way of weaning students away from the college experience. My colleagues and I lived and studied on campus during the summer months when the undergrad students were away. When the school year started up again, we were sent to cities across the country in groups of four to live and work. This way, we could remain connected in a real way to campus while also being invited to experience life "in the wild."

My years were spent in Houston, Texas, working at a relatively small (by Texas standards) parish downtown. I was grateful to not only live in a community of close colleagues, but also discover that the diocese had a vibrant young adult ministry. I remember I first met others in the group by showing up in a parking lot in response to a Facebook invitation to a Matt Maher concert. I jumped into a car packed with strangers to travel to the concert an hour away. I still laugh about that story because of how trusting (and sometimes naive) I really can be. Thankfully, this has not gotten me into any dangerous situations. If you don't get out of your comfort zone, it's going to be difficult to find a comfort zone that includes new friends.

Young adult groups provide many social activities to meet others in their 20s and 30s. As you know, a person's age in this range does not necessarily determine a state in life. This range runs the gamut of men and women who are single, dating, married (with and without kids) or divorced; student, graduate or workforce; local, transplant, or temporary resident of the city; and so many more characteristics. Sadly, the most pressure is put on those who are not in a relationship. The social situations with peers who share faith unintentionally turn into settings for matchmaking and dating. The drama that precedes or follows a fling or serious relationship in such a community can confuse its real purpose.

Though these groups are definitely rich soil for a healthy relationship to sprout with the shared faith and friendships, they can provide a much deeper message for those looking for meaning in their seasons. Whether someone gets married and is no longer an eligible bachelor or bachelorette or someone does not feel ready to date at that time, there is a need for encouragement and support. Since these groups are a part of Church ministry, the source of the confusion is the Church itself. As a leader in the Church myself, I had firsthand experience in the struggle of reaching a diverse mix of people with all different needs, preferences, and exceptions.

For the purpose of this book about what I've learned from being in the single season of life, I want to advocate for this population. A candid explanation is that the Church doesn't know what to do with us. I can guess that there are actually more of us in this season than ever before due to the increasing average age of saying "I do" at the altar and a longer life expectancy. Centuries ago, people typically chose a life path much earlier or had it chosen for them. So, though there is a delay in making vows in one direction or another, it is still important to recognize that the plan is still unfolding.

During this season as a single, 30-year-old woman in the Church, I have gained a new appreciation for this season and how it can witness to other vocations. As I savor this season of waiting on God, I am taught how to depend on Him above anything and anyone else. If I can't find happiness right where I am now, I will likely not find happiness in my next season. If God is not enough for me now, He won't be enough for me later. There is a powerful opportunity to be present in this transitional season.

As vocations require a lifelong commitment, time as a single person is valuable and to be cherished. Once you enter into matrimony, holy orders, or consecrated life, you are no longer single in the same way as before and will never be again. As a marriage therapist, I have recognized that the healthiest and happiest couples were happy and healthy on their own before they even met their partner. I pray that the Church can develop greater dialogue about this purposeful season on the way to sainthood. These important conversations will inspire discernment rather than expedite vows.

What I've learned about love as a single marriage counselor is that everyone is worthy of love and belonging no matter what season they're in, that all feelings are valid, and that love is the only thing that remains.

Reflection: How are you making the most out of your season right now? How can you be a gift for others in your season?

REFLECTION ON MY DATING FAST

As I finish this year-long dating fast in August 2019, I want to complete this book with a reflection on where I am today. I have been astounded by how God has worked in my life throughout this past year. When I began the fast in August 2018 and began writing this book in October 2018, I did not know how much I would discover about myself and my heart this year. I have stumbled across three conferences that taught me about how I can transform my story into a message, share it onstage, and communicate it with a more open and confident voice. I have joined accountability groups with other entrepreneurs and authors to build a business and publish this book. I have become a consultant for Arbonne, a skincare-product company, helping others improve their physical health. I have run my second half-marathon after eight years of thinking I was done after simply crossing my first one off of my bucket list. I have transitioned from working in a parish setting to focusing on my calling as a counselor. Stepping into a new position as a school-based therapist will help me to gain experience with elementary students and their parents while completing my full licensure!

God has had a tremendous number of surprises for me this year, and my heart has experienced healing and a readiness for what's ahead. Personally, I have learned that I have found my identity in relationships with family and friends rather than giving myself as a gift in those relationships. My identity is in God alone, and no matter where God leads me next or when my relationship status changes, I know I can fully experience joy right here where I am.

This book began as an antidote to my broken heart and now has grown into a wider message I want to share with the world. As a counselor, I hear many clients report feeling alone and being unclear about the purpose or direction of their life. I pray that this book has helped you to be assured in your heart that other hearts are longing and breaking like yours. Others wonder where their lives are headed or what to do in the meantime before transition comes. If anything, I am there with you in the valley, the ditch, or the desert as we journey toward the light, the beauty, and the comfort in the unknown. May you know how precious your life is.

Two years ago, I briefly became attracted to the idea of suicide. It felt dark around me and my world seemed destroyed. Now, I am aware that I experienced that darkness to develop an empathy for those who are feeling worthless, hopeless, or lost. One of the best ways to heal was to really focus on God's voice above the world's chatter and to recognize that life was happening for me rather than to me. Developing a more loving relationship with all pieces of my story helped me to embrace my story rather than let it define me. I have relationships, but I am not defined by them.

As I learn the power of sharing the stories that I don't really want to tell, I have found freedom and peace in accepting my seasons and what I have learned in each one. Seasons come, and seasons go, but all of them definitely help us to grow. You are being formed into the best person you can be, and I'm honored that you've welcomed me and my stories into your life through reading this book.

One of my favorite movies, *13 Going On 30*, features the Pat Benatar song "Love Is a Battlefield":

We are strong. Heartache to heartache we stand.
No promises, no demands. Love is a battlefield.

The world can make no promises, but Our Lord can. He is Love and fights for us and is alongside us in the battle. Though we know love wins in the end, we are warriors who will stand, defend, and proclaim the truth that each person is worthy of love. When we are face to face with our Maker in Heaven, we will no longer need faith or hope. Only love will remain. You are free to live loved right now.

PRAYER FOR THE SINGLE SEASON

Adapted from Psalm 119

Lord,

In this season of singleness, show me how much You love me. I want to seek You with my whole heart. Accompany my heart as I share with You my desire for a partner who can walk with me on my faith journey. As my Father, You want only the best for me, Your dear child. Please calm my fears and assure me of Your providence when I am filled with doubts. Shield me from temptation and discouragement. Help me to not wander from Your commands. Save me according to Your promise. Protect me from danger as I explore this world solo.

Speak through my loved ones as they support me in this season and give me the words to respond to any misunderstanding they might have. Enable me to speak the truth at all times and testify to all the good You have done in my life. Your testimonies are my delight. The presence of Your Spirit counsels and comforts me.

My hope is in You. You never put me to shame. Grant me perfect freedom to choose Your will. I find pleasure in obeying Your commands because I love them. I remember that I am nothing without Your spirit within me. I am made of dust and will return to dust. Grant me a spirit of detachment so that I don't grasp at anything that is worthless compared to You. You alone, Lord, satisfy my heart.

Have mercy on me, Lord, for the bad I have done and the good I have failed to do. In this season, please help me to be quick to serve You wholeheartedly whenever You call.

You are good and do only what is good. Even when my

condition doesn't look or feel good, You bring good out of all things. You are always teaching me and guiding me according to Your merciful and sacrificial love. You made me just the way I am and affirm that I am good. Help me to be a vessel so that others see You in me.

My soul longs for the love of a spouse here on earth. At times, I think You have forsaken me. How long will I wait on Your word? I am reminded of Your faithful promises and remember that I am Yours. I am Your servant; grant me a discerning mind that follows Your ways.

Accept my freely offered praise in the unknown. It sometimes feels like a stormy desert. When I encounter darkness, comfort me with Your presence. Your word is a lamp for my feet, a light for my path.

Let my soul live to praise You; may Your judgments give me help. I have wandered like a lost sheep. Come find me and draw me near. Though I come from a flock of other sheep, You pursue me. I am wonderfully made in Your sight. Hold me in Your arms so I can be comforted. I am a sojourner in this life who will forever be restless until I rest in You. Everything good in this life directs me home to You.

I call out to You with all of my heart.

You are near.

You are reliable.

You are refuge.

You are mine.

Love,
Your beloved

ACKNOWLEDGMENTS

Thank you to **all who have offered prayers and support** in this season. It has been an emotional roller coaster for sure. Thankfully with God's sense of humor, I overcame my lifelong fear of roller coasters before my breakup. Thank you to my dear **friends and family** who have listened to me, laughed with me, cried with me, and shared their honest feedback about my book and my life. I will be forever grateful for your presence in my life! You have helped me to find humor and truth in things and have challenged me to be humble, vulnerable, and honest about my own wounds. You have loved me through it all while validating my feelings, graciously affirming me, and teaching me to be perfectly imperfect.

Without my wounds, I wouldn't be able to experience the healing that the **Divine Physician** and **Divine Counselor** provides. Thank you, **Lord**, for being my steady shelter through the storm. You astonish me in Your daily pursuit of my heart as You prove again and again that true satisfaction is found only when I love You with my whole heart, soul, mind, and strength. Thank you for the living love letter You write me in Scripture and Your Body, Blood, Soul, and Divinity You share with me at Mass and in Eucharistic Adoration. May I always prioritize You in my heart and my schedule! Thank you to the **Saints** who have constantly interceded for me, especially the Holy Family. **Mary** and **Joseph** have taught me to ponder in my heart, wait on God, and live a life that points others to Christ.

Stephanie May Wilson, your "Love Your Single Life" course came at an ideal time following my breakup when I was at my lowest point. You helped me to gain a fresh perspective of the freedom in this season. **Natalie Met Lewis**, your singles devotionals have helped to guide my prayer life in this season, helped me live wholeheartedly, and always pointed me back to the love of my life in Christ. **Lysa TerKeurst** and **Rebekah Lyons**, your writing has taught me so much about how God meets us right where we are. I can bring my broken and anxious heart to the Father. **Emily Ley** and **Lara Casey**, your planners have helped to simplify my life and keep me focused on my goals in each season so I can continue to be my best self. **Brendon Burchard**, for inviting me to Experts Academy and awakening potential in my dreams and introducing me to **Bo Eason** and **Roger Love**. Bo and Roger have helped me to find my voice, recognize the power in my personal story, and the importance of sharing from the depths of my heart. **Rachel and Dave Hollis**, you bring so much joy and energy to my life. You encourage me to start each day with steps forward and not to compare my beginning with others' middles. Who doesn't need a daily declaration, "Let's gooooo!" Derek Jeter, for encouraging me from a young age to dream big and live the life I imagine.

Blessed is She, especially **Beth Davis**, who has taught me to embrace God's relentless love in singleness, and **Emily Wilson**, for speaking unapologetically about true love and advocating for a woman's heart in all seasons.

Self-Publishing School, for encouraging me on this adventure of making my dream of becoming an author come true. **Cheri Clark**, for your generous diligence in editing my manuscript. **Jed Jurchenko**, for coaching me each step of the way.

Clients for inviting me into your lives and teaching me more about love and for my phenomenal **therapist** for creating the space for me to explore my mind and heart.

ABOUT THE AUTHOR

Annie Harton, MA, LMFTA, works as a marriage and family counselor in her hometown of Indianapolis, Indiana. In addition to counseling, she enjoys diving deeper in her faith as a theologian, a catechetical leader, and an active parishioner at her downtown parish. She is always up for an adventure and finds delight in traveling. When she is at home, she can likely be found in the screened-in porch with Magdalene, her 2-year-old tiger cat, writing or reading. Her season of singleness has provided the space to learn to cook, dive into personal growth, and explore a hobby in photography. You can read her blog, see her photography portfolio, inquire about a speaking engagement, request prayer, and learn more at www.annieharton.com.

Made in the USA
Lexington, KY
22 September 2019